4/10/99

For Franny and Stephen,

Thank you for your
enduring love, friendship,
and support in every way,
including this book.
Love,
Francine
(and also Nicky)

CITY OF ONE

CITY OF ONE

A MEMOIR

Francine Cournos

W. W. NORTON & COMPANY • NEW YORK / LONDON

Excerpt from "East Coker" in *Four Quartets*, copyright 1943 by
T. S. Eliot and renewed 1971 by Esme Valerie Eliot, reprinted by
permission of Harcourt Brace & Company and
by permission of Faber & Faber Ltd.

Excerpt from *The Inferno*, translation by John Ciardi, copyright 1957,
1959, 1960, 1961 by John Ciardi, reprinted by permission of
W. W. Norton & Company, Inc.

The text of this book is composed in Goudy
with the display set in Engravers Bold
Composition by Platinum Manuscript Services
Manufacturing by Quebecor Printing, Fairfield, Inc.
Book design by Chris Welch

Library of Congress Cataloging-in-Publication Data

Cournos, Francine.
City of one : a memoir / by Francine Cournos.
p.   cm.
ISBN 0-393-04731-8
1. Cournos, Francine. 2. Physicians—United States—Biography.
3. Women psychiatrists—United States—Biography. I. Title.
RC438.6.C683   1999
610' .92—dc21
[B]   98–48136
CIP

W. W. Norton & Company, Inc., 500 Fifth Avenue, New York, N.Y. 10110
http://www.wwnorton.com

W. W. Norton & Company Ltd., 10 Coptic Street, London WC1A 1PU

1 2 3 4 5 6 7 8 9 0

For Helen C. Meyers and Daniel N. Stern

ACKNOWLEDGMENTS

The detailed work and constant attention of my husband, the writer Nicholas Bakalar, is reflected in every sentence of this book, and it would not exist without him.

Karen McKinnon persuaded me to undertake this project at a time when I had considerable doubt about it. She read and reread more drafts than I can count, offered extensive advice, and challenged me to express myself more clearly and directly. For all of this, I am indebted to her.

Richard Balkin provided guidance and support in measure

far outweighing any ordinary responsibilities of even the most conscientious literary agent, and has given me love and loyalty in measure far outweighing any ordinary responsibilities of even the most devoted friend.

In contrast to my relationship with my mother, my relationship with my daughter Elizabeth Bakalar is filled with words, and our exchanges are reflected in the details of this story, sometimes in ways that only she will recognize.

The gifted editors Deborah Brody, Carolyn Fireside, and Casey Fuetsch each took valuable time away from their own work to offer me specific comments on structure and wording. Elizabeth Tillinghast read the manuscript with a psychiatrist's expertise and helped me make essential psychological observations much more accurately.

James Bakalar, Kenneth Bakalar, Lee Bakalar, James Carey, Frances Cohen, Catherine Cooper, Alexis Cournos, Maureen Empfield, Jill Gully, Gerard Helferich, Richard Herman, Rachel Klayman, Stephen Koch, Mali Locke, Eric Marcus, Susan Milmoe, Wallace Nesby, Teresa Nicholas, Courtney Overland, Christina Sekaer, Phyllis Skolnik, David Strauss, Ezra Susser, Felice Swados, and Hank Wershaw read all or parts of the manuscript, and each provided useful suggestions and helpful encouragement.

There is a special group of people involved in the care of children orphaned by the HIV epidemic who inspired me in this project. Carol Levine was the first to suggest that I write about my experiences. She along with Jeffrey Blustein, Barbara Draiman, Nancy Dubler, Daniel Pilowsky, and Amy Shire and the other staff of the Family Center included me in their own projects and helped me to understand the potential value of telling my own story.

Lauren Graessle designed the jacket with perfect sensitivity to the book's spirit, and the keen-eyed Amy Robbins copyedited the manuscript with unstinting care. It is impossible to overstate the contribution of Jill Bialosky, my editor at Norton, relentless in her criticism, generous in her praise, tireless in her devotion to making this a better book. She is the kind of editor every writer wants, but most can only hope for.

Contents

12 Contents

CITY OF ONE

P R O L O G U E

M y mother never said good-bye to me. I stared out the
window at her receding figure, arm in arm with her
brother, and I thought: I may never see her again. I suspect
she knew she was never coming back. I had no name for her
condition, but this time was worse than the others. This time
she was barely able to breathe.

I am haunted by this parting: she said nothing to me as she
walked away. No "I love you," no "I'm sorry," no reassurance
that she was happy to care for us despite her debilitating illness, no instructions for what I was to do without her. Maybe

I wanted something impossible to give to an eleven-year-old, something that would sustain me for a lifetime, making up for all I would miss. Maybe she was too sick to say good-bye. Maybe she was too upset to confront the end. I will never know, nor will I ever stop wondering.

This is an account of loss and reconnection that begins with my earliest memories and ends in the present. I have recorded the facts just as I remember them, using written documentation whenever it was available. It is also, to be sure, a subjective account, told from an internal perspective, first that of a child, later that of a young woman and a physician practicing internal medicine, and finally that of a psychiatrist.

I was born in the 1940s, the middle of three children. We lived in the South Bronx, a lower-middle-class neighborhood of Irish, Italians, and Jews. The family considered my mother's first husband a useless bum, allergic to real work, wasting his time writing unpublishable novels, and when Mom accidentally got pregnant after ten years of marriage, he wanted her to have an abortion. Instead, she left him and had the baby, and in less than the two years that separated my brother's birth from mine, she divorced her first husband and married my father. My mother was thirty-seven, my father fifty-four. Dad, who worked as a proofreader for the *New York Times* while my mother stayed home with us, seemed to have no family, no past at all that I could discern until I was an adult. I remember almost nothing of what I take to be these idyllic years with my nuclear family, because soon the adults in my life began to disappear, one by one. By the time I was a teenager, I was living with strangers in a foster home.

Here are the bare facts of my childhood. I was three years old when my father suddenly died from a cerebral hemorrhage caused by an undiagnosed brain tumor. My half brother was five, and my mother was two months pregnant with my younger sister. My father had been the sole wage earner, and had left little money. My mother's parents moved in with her to help out with finances and child care. Two years later, my grandfather died suddenly when he hemorrhaged from a peptic ulcer. Shortly after that, my mother developed breast cancer, which soon metastasized. She lived until I was eleven, undergoing multiple surgeries and other disfiguring treatments. I watched her body and my world disintegrate as she became increasingly ill and our neighborhood—the South Bronx—became a violent ghetto. For two years following my mother's death, we continued to live with our grandmother, who, now approaching senility, took care of us until she no longer could. Then my mother's siblings placed my younger sister and me together in foster care. I was thirteen, my sister was nine. My half brother was already living in a residential school, and we gradually lost all contact with him.

In the beginning of my attempt to put this unraveled life back together, I was driven by a powerful delusion: I had caused what had happened to me, and I had to set things right. This idea, combined with an ability to escape from real life by burying myself in books, sustained me through college and medical school. It did not occur to me that going to medical school would change me from an indigent foster child into a respectable member of the upper middle class. Making a living was not what interested me. I was absorbed in a fight against death, and especially against the death of my mother.

Practicing medicine gave me some understanding of the exquisite mechanisms by which the body works, and my childhood confusion about how a person crosses the line between life and death gradually dissolved.

I was a year away from completing my residency in internal medicine when, while working on a cancer ward, I was finally able to acknowledge that there was nothing I could do to bring my mother back, or to save anyone else with the type of breast cancer that took her life. But in the meantime I had discovered something new: the possibility of discussing the frightening feelings my mother and I had so sedulously avoided mentioning. That is when I switched to psychiatry.

I found my patients' perspectives compelling, as I still do, but it was primarily in the context of my own psychotherapy and psychoanalysis that I focused on my losses, my feelings of depression, and my ever-present fear of betrayal. Treatment had a profoundly positive impact on my life, and I looked to psychiatric writings to uncover what mysterious theory or practice had such a powerful effect on me.

I found that while a great deal has been written about the impact of parental death in childhood, much remains unknown. A small number of rigorous scientific studies show that children are adversely affected in a variety of ways. But the most moving accounts of childhood mourning can be found in the psychoanalytic literature. Here, the authors draw their observations from their work with patients to create theories about how children handle death. One of the central themes in this literature is whether children can mourn like adults: can they surrender the lost parent and move on? Healthy adult mourning involves a gradual and painful detachment from the person who has died, followed by the freedom to make substitute attachments, and many analytic writers conclude that children may have to pass through adolescence before this kind of mourning is possible.

But as I read, I wondered why anyone would want to measure children against an adult standard in the first place. If children and their caretakers so often fail to resolve a parent's death in some hypothetically healthy process, maybe it is because there is usually neither a truly ideal method a child can use nor a corresponding ideal family to provide help and guidance in the process. Moreover, most papers I read focused on children in treatment who face a situation in which one parent has died and the remaining parent and family are still available. How about children with no parents, or those who never find adequate parental substitutes? If one loss can be devastating, how is this to be distinguished from a series of losses, each exacting its own agonizing toll?

It is probably a mistake to use outside appearances to judge a child's success in such matters. By the time both my parents were dead, when I was eleven, I knew how to defend myself against physical threats in my neighborhood, I could shop for food, repair clothes on a sewing machine, accomplish all my schoolwork without any adult prompts, and take care of my seven-year-old sister. Between eleven and thirteen, when I lived with my grandmother, who was illiterate and spoke no English, I became the reader, translator, and negotiator in our interactions with the outside world. In high school, I was an honor student and worked twenty hours a week to pay some of my own expenses.

I acted, in effect, like a miniature adult. But underneath the bravado and the cool competence was a very needy child who suffered from depression, self-hatred, distrust of adults, an inability to make any new intimate connections, and a tremendous loss of a sense of structure. In short, I was not what I appeared to be.

I became an orphan in 1956, when having two parents die was very unusual. Sadly, this is no longer so. With the onset of the HIV epidemic, losing both parents has become an increasingly common event of childhood in many parts of the country. Of course, no two children would tell the same story. Even my own siblings, whose experience I barely discuss here, would give very different subjective accounts if they were describing these same events. And I have no illusion that the solutions I found will work for anyone else. I was never exposed to physical abuse, drug addiction, war, or many of the other conditions of extreme deprivation that rip children's lives apart today. Yet children who have experienced significant loss, whether of one parent or both, have much in common. I hope that in telling my own story, I will make some small contribution to helping people understand what children face in these circumstances.

There are risks for a psychiatrist in writing a book like this. In my work with patients I do not engage in self-revelation— there is almost always a more useful strategy in helping patients solve their problems. Moreover, I am inclined by my own nature to avoid talking publicly about my background, to maintain the silence and privacy I found so important as a child, and to remain known to my patients only as their doctor. But I hope that sharing my experiences will make the book useful enough to others to be worth the risks involved in writing it.

When I think about my losses and what followed, I find

there is no clear starting point for my troubles, nor any permanent resolution. Each stage of life reawakens old memories that need to be faced yet again, and the trauma of early parental loss reasserts itself in different forms throughout a lifetime. No matter what his or her age or particular circumstances, almost everyone who has suffered a parent's death agrees with this: if your parent dies when you are still a child, the loss endures forever.

Chapter 1

DISAPPEARANCES

(1948–1953)

I stared down her housedress as she bent over to bathe me. One breast moved with the motion of her scrubbing me. Where the other would have been, there was just a scar. Something frightening had happened; I just didn't know what. I could see the evidence—the bandages covering one part of her body and then another, the swollen arm—and I furtively examined the padded bras in her drawer. But I remained mystified.

As a child, I was preoccupied with things that disappeared, but my mother's breast was what I noticed most, its absence an inescapable reminder of what was no longer. This was an essential mystery, one I could not solve, and whose contemplation led only to a fear of what might disappear next.

My mother and I never talked about her missing breast. I don't know if I was scared to ask her, or if I sensed that talking didn't suit her and I was trying not to upset her. Once in a while, I got up the courage to ask about something. "Why is your arm all swollen up?" Mom said it was because of her operation, but I really didn't understand what a missing breast had to do with a swollen arm. Mom sort of joked about how she looked with two arms that didn't match. I loved both her arms, the fat one and the skinny one, but I couldn't help thinking that something had gone terribly wrong.

We didn't talk about my father, either. He had vanished with barely a trace when I was three. No picture of him existed in our house. No member of his family was present in our lives. For the brief time he was sick, I stayed with my Aunt Milly at a rented summer cottage. I was lost, wandering on an immense, beautifully manicured lawn, crying for my parents. I was all alone, but Aunt Milly found me. After that, Dad never showed up again, and Mom never spoke of him. Once in a while, one of my aunts would make some complimentary reference to him. "Your father loved children. If he was walking down the street and a child had a runny nose, he would stop to wipe it." Dad had worked at night as a proofreader for the *New York Times*. "He was so considerate, when he came home from work he would take off his shoes and tiptoe into the bedroom so he wouldn't wake your mother up." And sometimes they would say, "He was much older than your mom," a remark to which in time I silently added the words I imagined they left out: "So no wonder he died and left her all alone with three children."

I have three memories of my father.

I'm sitting behind my father on the edge of the bathtub watching him shave. Our eyes meet in the mirror in a moment of total mutual adoration. I am entranced by the careless grace with which he carries out the morning ritual that for me defines his masculinity. And I can see how pleased he is to have his very own little girl.

My father is sitting at the kitchen table, and my brother and I are competing to climb into his lap. In the end, we both get a piece of him, my brother ascending one leg, me the other.

The bathroom door is slightly ajar and I peek in to see my father teaching my brother to pee standing up. They take aim. I'm about to enter when my mother pulls me back and indicates that I'm not part of this. But I want to learn to pee standing up, too! I feel left out, excluded.

Gradually I wove these three memories into my own private theories. Being an adorable girl had not been enough to hold on to my father. No, I would have to compete with boys, be just as good as them, and, of course, outdo my brother Henry. And then, if I still couldn't get my father back, I could preserve him within me by being just like him, replace him as Mom's most devoted helper and favorite companion, show how well we could manage without him, and prove I was just as good as kids who still had a father. My extravagant theories seemed much better than admitting that the loss was permanent and harmful, that Dad was irreplaceable and irretrievable, and that I would just have to finish growing up without him.

My father was dead, my half brother Henry was five years old, I was just turning three, and my mother was two months pregnant. Shortly before the new baby was born, I was sitting next to Mom on the living room couch. She said, "Feel this," and put my hand on her stomach. Thump! What was that? Mom said it was the baby kicking. One person inside another! This remarkable encounter was my first meeting with my baby sister Alexis.

When Mom brought Alexis home, I somehow picked that moment to fall out of my crib and hurt my back. I was lying on the living room couch nursing my injuries when they walked in. "Mom, I fell out of my crib and I hurt myself." Mom was carrying Alexis, and she ignored me. When my demands became too much for her, she paid no attention at all. By the time she got mad, you knew things had gone entirely too far.

Alexis, born seven months after Dad died, was the closest thing to a reminder of our father, Alexander. If Dad had not died, she would have been Lydia, which became her middle name. Since neither Henry nor I had a middle name, I figured this was something extra Alexis got, compensation for never meeting Dad, not even once.

But if Mom could produce a new person with Dad's name, was she then responsible for his disappearance in the first place? I couldn't quite grasp how this replacement had happened, but I feared Mom possessed some ineffable power, and each subsequent disruption served to increase my wariness.

Losing a father so young left me with little sense of loyalty to him, so being fickle seemed no problem. Every new man who came along became the next opportunity to replace him. Grandpa was my next true love. He and Grandma moved in with us to help Mom after Dad died. Grandpa, bald and stout, worked in a haberdashery. I loved the moment when he came home every evening, because you could never tell what hat he would be wearing. "Grandpa, how come you have so many hats?" I'd ask, and I would stare at him admiringly as he answered, always smiling: "Because I work in a haberdashery." That wonderful word again, rolling off his lips.

We lived in the Bronx, on the second floor of a four-story building. Our apartment went all the way through from the front to the back, six big rooms with lots of furniture. Right next door was a little plot of grassy land where tombstones were sold. It looked so much like a cemetery that it was hard to believe no one was buried there. One block away was Bathgate Avenue, a jumbled array of bustling stores and outdoor stands selling what seemed to me the entire universe of imaginable things. Just one block more and you came to Crotona Park: a huge expanse of trees, walkways, and benches, a playground, and a swimming pool.

Mom's family all lived nearby. She was the oldest of four children—there were two more girls, and then finally a boy. My Aunt Lillian worked for the Bulova watch company, and sometimes she had chest pains, but I didn't know why she'd chosen to marry the monstrous Hy, big, swarthy, and scary with dark brown eyes that stared with cold disapproval. I did my best to stay as far away as possible, and fortunately he had little interest in me. Next came Anne, the family beauty, who had red hair and worked as a waitress. She didn't like it when customers tried to save money by ordering a bowl of plain broth and then putting their own pieces of chicken in to make soup with it—they would leave her only a five-cent tip. She was married to my favorite uncle, Jack, who worked as a chef. At family dinners he did the cooking with a happy-go-lucky demeanor that set him apart, as if he'd arrived from some alternate universe and hadn't yet learned to be discontented like the rest of us. But his cooking was delicious, and you could get all the tastes you wanted while he was working—he never said you'd lose your appetite. He was very sweet, quite a contrast, from what I had heard, to Anne's first husband. I never met him, but he was even meaner than Uncle Hy, and sometimes even used to beat Anne, or so the story went when anyone was willing to tell it. Finally, there was poor timid, bald Milton, always being bossed around by his wife Milly, always trying to please her, always failing. It was painful to watch, and sometimes I wished he'd just stand up to her and stop being such a sissy.

When I was five, Grandpa disappeared just as suddenly as Dad. Lots of grown-ups came by and sat in the living room while I wandered around the apartment, everyone ignoring me. He died of a bleeding ulcer in his stomach, they said. I imagined blood gushing into Grandpa's stomach, but I wasn't sure why that would make someone die. I heard one of the visitors mention that before you die, you change color. That was a clue. I went into the bathroom and stood on the toilet seat so I could secretly stare into the mirror to check my color, fearing pink, or blue, or chartreuse. I was relieved to find myself the usual color, but for years after that I kept checking just to be certain. Surely children don't just disappear without warning, do they?

It seemed there was no one to talk to, so I went to my bedroom and lay there, curled up on top of the covers, facing the wall, worrying about what happens to people after they die. The idea of life after death seemed horrible. Suppose it was as boring and disconnected as things were right this minute, except that I wouldn't be able to escape the feeling because I'd be dead, and of course there is no escape from being dead. No, it's better if there is no heaven and everything just ends.

I was five years old, isolated from the adults in mourning around me. I felt painfully estranged, an inconsequential speck. As an adolescent, I was amazed to discover that the term "existential despair" was the label for this condition, and that my feelings were only peculiar in having started so young and persisted so long. It wasn't until middle age that I finally managed to create a world in which I believed it was both safe and realistic to feel significant.

Just after Grandpa died, Mom went into the hospital for her first operation. Henry hadn't taken well to any of this, and he didn't plan to hide his feelings like the rest of us. Henry had always been eager to attract attention. He had thick brown hair and big blue eyes and liked to strut around like a movie star, singing "Oh, my papa, to me you were so wonderful" to any audience willing to listen, and to Alexis and me even when we weren't. It took me a long time to figure out that Henry had a different father—since he'd forgotten all about Henry and almost never came to visit. Henry liked to parade around naked to show us he had a penis and we didn't. But his angry excursions into imaginative new kinds of mischief were more than Mom could abide. He set off firecrackers, fought with other kids, played mean tricks that made Alexis and me cry, spent his milk money on candy so that the school had to write to Mom to ask why he never had money for milk. Henry was just one too many things for Mom to handle. She sent him to a foster home. "What's it like there?" I asked him one weekend when he was home visiting.

"I live in a basement. They don't give me enough to eat. They feed me with the dog." I was sorry for Henry, but a little relieved that he wasn't around to torment me, then guilty that I found even small satisfaction in his misfortune. And, of course, I had to consider whether Mom might send me away next. I could not fathom how the mother who yelled and screamed at Henry was the same one who was so calm and patient with me. It felt like Henry was gone forever, but years later his foster-care records would show that he lived there for six months, when he was seven years old. Finally, Mom took Henry back. When he returned, they still fought. I implored Henry not to provoke Mom, and covered up for him when I could, trying to believe this helped a little.

Mom had to work now, because someone had to make money. I spent my days in nursery school, a vast room filled with kids and toys, interesting enough for the most part, except for the moments I stopped feeling any connection to my new surroundings, overcome by the same sense of estrangement I had when Grandpa died. One spring Sunday, Mom took us on a Circle Line cruise—the tourist boat ride that begins at a pier on the Hudson River. I stood out on the deck of the huge boat, where I could see the water and the skyline and feel the breeze on my face. The ride lasted a long time, and when we came into shore, Mom took my hand to disembark. "Why are we getting off here? Don't we have to go back to the other side where we came from?"

I was thinking we'd crossed over, and now we had to go back. "But we are back," said Mom, and then, when I remained incredulous, she drew me a picture. "We went in a circle, like this," she said, penciling the outline of Manhattan on the scrap of paper and indicating our route. I had no idea what she was talking about. As far as I was concerned, we'd gone in a straight line and landed on another shore, the opposite bank. Since I was completely baffled by Mom's explanation, I made up my own: while we were gone, the whole world reversed itself. We used to live on one side of the water, but now we lived on the other side. The world had simply turned itself inside out.

The event weighed on my mind. Why doesn't the world stay as it is? As soon as I learned to read, I began to try to figure things out. I sought answers for my questions in books: Why does it rain? Why does sound come out of a radio? Where does electricity come from? How do whirlpools form?

I was afraid of disappearing into a whirlpool. If I fell into one, I'd get sucked down and drown and never come up again. The idea of quicksand gave me the same shudder of fear, so I was careful where I walked. I knew from the radio that children disappear into wells all over the place—like little Chrissie who fell into a well in Texas and stayed there for twenty-two hours until the rescuers got her out.

I went to the movies to see *Fantasia*. One broom carrying a pail of water starts to multiply, and pretty soon there are hundreds of them, all carrying buckets, and so much water that it makes a gigantic flood—I sat in the dark, terrified by the thought of being unable to get a breath of air. I took a swimming test. I'd been doing well in the shallow water, but to pass I had to go into the deep water. I jumped in, started to sink, and became paralyzed with the fear that I would suffocate. Someone had to rescue me. Even a broken water faucet scared me. What if they never came to fix it, and the water never stopped, and we all drowned?

Losing things always worried me. I was playing outside with my friends when a tooth fell right out of my mouth. I was bleeding and I started to cry. I ran upstairs, "Mom, my tooth fell out!" I was panicked—what else might fall out? Mom reminded me that I was getting big, and that my baby teeth would fall out and I'd get new ones. Now I remembered—of course!—and I felt embarrassed for crying like a baby.

Once I got lost in Crotona Park. Mom was tending to Alexis when I ran down the stairs and out of the park, restless for a new activity. I couldn't find my way back, so I began to wail. A passing police car stopped. "What's wrong, little girl?" The two very nice policemen let me get in the backseat of their car and we drove around searching for Mom. I was inconsolable, convinced that because I'd carelessly wandered off, I would never see her again. To cheer me up, the policeman handed me a giant bag of chocolates, which I proceeded to gobble up, one by one, crying all the while. "There she is!" Mom had left the park to search for me, and I had finally found her. I immediately lost all interest in the nice policemen, but by this time I had eaten every last chocolate.

Disaster never seemed far away. My pink rubber ball rolled into the street and I raced after it. As I bent down to pick it up, I heard a terrible screeching sound right behind me. Ball in hand, I turned around, and there was a bus, not two inches away from me. My God, the driver really made an effort not to kill me! My heart was beating—with sinking fear, blessed relief, and painful guilt at my carelessness all at once. How many times could I escape death? When would my luck run out? Once Mom and I were coming back from shopping and we were standing on the corner waiting for the green light when a little old lady walked up behind me. "Let the lady go first," Mom said. Just as I did, a car came screeching around the corner, skidded right onto the sidewalk, and ran over the lady—right where I had been standing a moment before. Mom saved me! I tried not to look at the mangled body lying in the street. It was gory and terrifying, and it was almost me.

But whatever I could not bear to know and look at as a child, I would feel compelled to pursue as an adult.

It is more than twenty years later, and I'm the medical resident in charge of the emergency room when they bring the old woman in. She was crossing the street in front of the hospital when a car ran her over. The driver fled, leaving her bleeding in the road. We bring her in on a stretcher and lift her onto the examining table. Only then do we discover that her right leg has nearly been severed from her torso; her femoral artery is pumping blood all over the table and onto the floor. We descend, trying to clamp the artery while simultaneously transfusing blood into her to try to replace what she's losing. Her heart keeps pumping, pumping her blood onto the soaked sheets with grim efficiency. She stares right at us, stunned, wordless, but slowly her eyes shut and she loses consciousness. Within a few minutes, she has bled to death despite the swirling frenetic activity of the doctors around her. As I watch her die, a wave of nausea comes over me, and I am not alone: I see my own pale reflection in the faces of my colleagues. I have become familiar with death, learned to look squarely at it. I have figured out how to practice a physician's objectivity in the face of things that once paralyzed me. But every once in a while, the old fear and horror and revulsion overtake me.

I knew Mom wasn't banishing me the first time she sent me to sleep-away camp when I was six years old, but I was scared anyway. You weren't allowed to bring your own clothes, and that now familiar feeling of detachment began to blossom as I watched counselors count out the camp-issue socks, shorts, and T-shirts. We stood on line for everything: to get clothes, to shower, to eat. A large semicircle of identical cabins was set on a huge lawn. I panicked when I couldn't figure out which one was mine. My mother, undaunted, tried another camp the next summer, and this time she found a place I loved.

Masonic Camp Seven became my favorite part of summer. It was run by the Masons, whoever they were, and it was only for girls. I got to go for three weeks, and we sang, and played, and put on shows. Every day at rest hour I wrote my mother a letter. The moment of greatest suspense occurred when the counselor distributed the mail. When a letter or postcard arrived from Mom, which it did most days, I was thrilled, and when there was none, I fought the profound feeling of disappointment. Sometimes she sent me something really special—like new stationery or the *Weekly Reader*, a four-page newspaper for kids. I learned, after all, to enjoy being away from her. When the three weeks ended and it was time to go home, I was nervous at the bus stop, unsure if Mom was going to meet me, or if she was sick or at work and had sent someone else. And still later I'd wonder if it was during some moment in the summer when I allowed time to pass without thinking about Mom, let my need for her lapse, that I created the opening through which she slipped and forever disappeared.

Back home, the same frightening things were still going on, but Mom and I did not talk about them. Most of our relationship didn't depend on words. Really, I was old enough to bathe myself, but I loved the feeling of my mother's hands on me, gently washing my arms and legs. I liked how she set out my clothes every morning (except for the one ugly gray dress I hated to wear). I loved when she combed my hair, making it just right with the colorful plastic barrettes she used to keep it from falling in my face. If my clothes got dirty, Mom changed them all over again. She liked me to look pretty, and she even took me to her beauty parlor. I had thick, thick hair, and the lady cut it with a special scissors. I felt very grown-up.

Mom loved it when I scratched her back and tickled her feet. I touched her arms as if I could feel the thousands of freckles that dotted the upper surfaces. She had auburn hair and blue eyes—everyone said I took after my darker-complected dad, but I couldn't picture what he looked like. I admired Mom in her fancy dress and high-heeled shoes, decorated with jewelry, perfumed and made-up, ready to go out on Saturday night, and I loved the snack she prepared for us before she left. Three little bags on the kitchen counter, one for each of us, containing our favorite foods: almonds, dried apricots, and chocolate. Then we watched TV while we ate, and I knew she was thinking about us even though she wasn't home. And in the middle of the night, when I had bad dreams, Mom didn't mind if I woke her to comfort me.

Sometimes I kept Mom company when she was busy with housework. She was ironing the clothes when a popular song came on the radio. We were singing along, and then instead of Mom singing "Is it all going in one ear and out the other?" which is how it was supposed to go, she sang, "Is it all going in one ear and out the earmuffs?" I started to laugh, and then Mom laughed, and then we laughed even harder, and soon I was laughing so hard my stomach was aching, so I lay down on the floor and just went on laughing to the point of exhaustion. I have almost never experienced these extended moments of uncontrolled, pure delighted laughter in adulthood, but they happened often when I was a child. Mom hung Henry's pajamas on the clothesline to dry, but it was winter, and when she brought them in, they were frozen. This was funny enough, but when she accidentally dropped them, they broke in two! General stomach-clutching hilarity ensued.

One day we visited the observatory at the Empire State Building. For thirty-five cents you could make your own three-minute record. Please, Mom, please! She gave in. Alexis and I started to sing "If All the Rain Drops Were Lemon Drops and Gum Drops," but as the time began running out, our squeaky little voices went faster and faster, and we never did get to finish, and the record ends stuck on the words "gum drops, gum drops, gum drops. . . ." If you let it, the record will say that forever. But our singing was not the best part anyway. The best part was when Mom said, "Speak into the microphone," her words forever etched there, so that long after she was gone I could still hear the sound of her voice instructing us, trying to make it come out right.

But despite the many ways my mother cared for and protected me, despite my attempts to make logical sense of how things disappeared, I still believed in bad magic. Lacking any way to grasp the idea that things could happen over which even powerful adults had no control, I watched warily for Mom's evil intentions, and secretly worried that she was purposely making things vanish. She tried to give me an enema because I was constipated. Standing naked in the white porcelain bathtub, I refused to let her near me, screaming as loud as I could at her approach. No one was going to steal my insides! Mom never tried that one again, but I kept up my guard. I went to the movies and saw Snow White. When I came home, Mom had made mushroom soup. She's never made that before, I thought suspiciously. My own version of Snow White played on the movie screen in my mind. Once upon a time, it began, a little girl lived with her older brother and her baby sister and her mother, who seemed to be pretty nice, at least most of the time. But scary things kept happening in this house; people kept disappearing, one by one. So the little girl wanted to make sure she didn't disappear, too! I refused even to taste Mom's soup. She got annoyed and insisted I couldn't leave the table before finishing, but I knew that if I ate that stuff, I'd be dead. I wasn't going to eat it even if she made me sit there for the rest of my life. I had nothing to lose: I'd sit there forever, I'd never eat or sleep again, I'd never go to school. Faced with this kind of determination, Mom could do nothing but admit defeat. But by the time the next meal came around, I'd completely forgotten about poisoned soup. And the normal developmental task of integrating the good and bad images of my mother was one I would not achieve as a child. My fear that Mom wanted to harm me was just as alive as my love and admiration for how hard she struggled to take care of us, and I made no attempt to resolve the contradiction.

One day, when I was six years old, good magic happened: Mom picked me up at nursery school and we went outside and walked down the three stone steps to the sidewalk. I looked up, and there he was, a stranger waiting to meet me.

"This is my friend Sam," Mom said, but by the way he smiled at me I could tell that this was no ordinary friend. This was Mom's new man, and for me, it was love at first sight. A warm, familiar feeling came over me, as if someone important had returned.

After that, I looked forward to every weekend, because that's when Sam came to visit. He had thick, wavy gray hair, and the beginnings of wrinkles on his face. His voice was rich and deep with a heavy foreign accent, and his fingers were stained yellow from smoking Camel cigarettes one after the other. Sam's name was really Salvatore. He was from Italy, which was someplace in Europe. He liked anchovies on his pizza. I hated anchovies, but I adored Sam. He was a house-painter and plasterer, and he couldn't read or write, just like Grandma. He was a lot older than Mom. Sam let me sit on his lap, examine his discolored fingers, and decorate his hair with my pretty bows and barrettes. Mom told me to stop doing that, I guess because men don't need decorations in their hair. But I loved to feel Sam's hair, and Sam didn't mind, so I kept right on with the game.

Every so often we went to visit Sam at his house. That's how I learned that Sam lived with his mother, which seemed odd for a grown man. The apartment was tiny, crowded with dozens of statues of the Virgin Mary placed on little white doilies on every table and dresser, crucifixes and pictures of Jesus on every wall. In one, Christ had stakes through his hands and legs, and drops of blood flew through the air in gory little arcs. I wondered why anyone would want such a gruesome picture hanging where you have to see it all the time. I sat there quietly—there was hardly room to move, and I was afraid that if I did, I'd knock over one of the statues and break it.

My school was near Crotona Park. First I would take Alexis to nursery school, where she spent the day, and then I walked the five blocks to P.S. 4, all with no help from Mom. I learned a new word in class: posthumous. "Alexis! Guess what! There's a special word for what happened to you," I told my sister. "You were born posthumously, after your father died, and that's what they call it." It surprised me that there was a label for what happened to Alexis, and now I could see it wasn't so peculiar after all. I felt sure Alexis would be delighted to know that she was not alone, that it had happened so often they'd invented a word for it. But after I told her, she only looked at me quizzically—I could see that her enthusiasm for being a member of this group was limited.

After school I usually went to my best friend Sarah's house. Sarah's mom didn't work, so she was always home waiting for us with cookies and milk and chocolate syrup. In Sarah's apartment building lived two families, one with four boys, one with four girls. Each mother was pregnant, hoping, hoping for a baby of a different sex. When they each, true to form, produced the same sex they always produced, my first thought was: Why not just trade babies? Then everyone will have what they want. Of course, I realized it wasn't so easy to switch— you couldn't just insert a different kid into a family, any more than you could insert a new father when you'd lost the one you had.

Sometimes I was there when Sarah's dad came home. His name was Julius, and he was a lithographer, but we had no idea what he actually did all day. He was very patient and gentle, and smart, too. Sarah's parents hid in Europe during World War II so they wouldn't get killed like most Jewish people did. They were lucky to have lived, and Sarah was lucky to have them. She shared her parents with me, or at least that's how I felt when I visited. One day I spilled choco- late syrup all over the floor and her mother came in and start- ed to yell. Sarah immediately said that she had done it. I couldn't believe she was taking the blame for me. I should have spoken up and admitted my carelessness, but I was so afraid of falling out of her mother's good graces that I just said nothing, feeling silently grateful to Sarah. I never heard her dad yell, not even once. I wished he was my dad, too.

By dinnertime I headed off to the Jewish Ladies Day Nursery, which was for kids whose mothers worked. The food there was not too good, and Sylvia, who was very fat and bossy, tried to make us eat it all up. I had no intention of submitting, but opposition to Sylvia the scary witch-mother required a covert operation. My technique for dealing with food I preferred not to eat was to stealthily stick it in my shoe. Suppose they were serving mashed potatoes with spinach mixed in, a stomach-turning combination if ever there was one. I was seated with seven other children, and Sylvia was on patrol, roaming from table to table. When she was looking elsewhere (and when no children could see either—they can tell on you), I would grab the gushy potatoes with my right hand and stick them in the back of my shoe. Then I would casually raise my left hand to ask to go to the bathroom. Walking on my toes to avoid squashing the potatoes (but not so much on my toes as to look suspicious), I would make my way to safety. There, I would flush the evidence down the toilet, clean out my shoe, dry it with paper towels, and coolly return to the scene of the crime. Once you learned to do this with mashed potatoes, string beans and carrots were easy.

It was there that I learned the facts of life. I was nine when some of the other girls told me, and I couldn't believe such a preposterous story, because you wouldn't think something a man uses to pee with could be used for such an entirely different purpose. Jill was the first to get breasts, but I was the first to have pubic hair. I know, because we all compared anatomies in the bathroom.

Sometimes it seemed fine being a girl, but other times I wished I was a boy. I loved to put on my dungarees and polo shirt and climb steep rocks and scale fences. I especially liked the fence around Crotona Park, black metal slats about four feet high, topped with a flat metal strip perfect for tight-rope walking. Except one time I slipped, landing painfully with one leg on each side of the fence. I hoped that landing hadn't ruined my virginity! I once heard a story about a girl who got married, and her membrane was already broken, so she didn't bleed on her wedding night and her husband gave her back. When we took an aptitude test in school, it showed I was the only girl in the class who wanted to grow up to be a mechanic. If I were a boy, I thought, I could marry a woman who would take care of me while I did something important—like discovering a cure for a disease. And I knew how to fight. Once I got into a brawl with two boys, and I won.

But other times I just wanted to snuggle with boys, especially with Henry's friend Benjamin, who was a little fat and very cuddly. And then there was dancing for Sam. Alexis and I would wear nothing but our underpants and gossamer scarves to carry out our little performances.

Sometimes I disguised myself so that no one could tell what sex I was. The white sheet draped over me was a boring ghost costume for a Halloween Day parade, but the pleasing part was that no one could figure it out—was I a boy or a girl? In my mind, I liked to pretend I could be both—an adorable girl when a handsome man was around, and a competent boy when I realized that I had to take care of myself and my mom without a man to help.

Of course, when I was acting like a boy, it was important to be a little bossy. At school, I was class president. And then after school I rummaged through the closets at the Jewish Ladies Day Nursery, gathered my art supplies, and then announced my own art classes, as if I'd been authorized to step into the role of the teacher. I was the gardener there, too. I invented that job by bringing seeds and planting them in the little bits of dirt that surrounded the concrete of our playground. Then, on hot summer days when I had to be there because there was no place else to be, and the dreaded rest hour came, I got to excuse myself and water my seedlings and fuss over the bigger plants so they'd look just right.

Naturally, when Alexis was with me I had to instruct her in everything. For the most part, I was nice to her, but sometimes I wondered if it was right to make her play horse and carriage by looping a rope around her waist and having her drag me around on my roller skates, all the while giving her little candy pellets to help her keep up her energy. When I saw something interesting lying on the street, I would yell "Whoa-oa-oa!" and stop to inspect. Once I collected a handful of shiny little hard brown beans. I had a feeling my brother would try to take them from me, so I hid them under a rock in front of our apartment building. A week later, I came back to get them and picked up the rock: no beans! Instead, about twenty little seedlings slowly righted themselves as I watched! I was sad to lose my beans—and maybe a little embarrassed for not realizing that they were seeds. But neither of those emotions was as powerful as my astonishment at the spunkiness of these little seedlings, growing like that under a rock and then standing up straight as soldiers as soon as they had the chance!

Finally, I would be back home again, and remember that Mom was sick, so I strove to be the helpful child. This was my special role. Henry got to be the troublemaker: Mom was always getting mad at him for something. And Alexis was the adorable baby—she was sweet and quiet, and oh, what pretty eyes she had! Everyone said so! Mom had a special set of pictures of her—just the two of them sitting on a park bench on a beautiful spring day. Henry and I didn't have pictures with Mom. But I did get to be Mom's most devoted helper, and I was much more loyal than Grandma, who went to that rundown part of Miami Beach where all the old Jewish ladies gathered every winter, leaving Mom and me to be the responsible ones.

But my longing for more attention from fatherly men stayed with me. One day a really nice man stopped me and asked for my help. I remembered Mom's warnings: Never go with strangers. But this man seemed so kind. And I had to admit his offer of fifteen cents was very tempting. With that much money, I could buy three big candy bars! So I followed him up a flight of stairs to the second story of an apartment building where, he said, I should help him look for his friend on the roof. He picked me up and I peered through a crack at the top of a heavy metal door out onto a small piece of tarred rooftop. But while I was doing that, I felt his hand slip into my underpants and he touched me. I felt a shiver of fear. "Put me down now! I have to go!" He immediately released me and I started to run away. "Wait! Your fifteen cents!" he shouted. And he was true to his word: he gave me the coins. I took them, but the money seemed tainted and dirty, so when I got home, I put it away instead of spending it on the candy I had dreamed of. I felt guilty because I hadn't listened to Mom, and very worried, because I wondered if a man touches you like that maybe you get damaged. I wished Mom could reassure me, but provoking the wrath of someone who could make people disappear seemed much too risky. Besides, I was too ashamed to tell anyone. The worry persisted: I shouldn't have done that, and now I was irreparably changed.

I'm listening to a senior psychiatrist comment on a case I have just presented. "Little girls without fathers," he says, "are more likely to be molested. They're tempted by the attention of men who are strangers." My mind wanders back to the man with the fifteen cents. No, I want to protest, we are not more vulnerable than little girls who still have fathers. I feel compelled to alternate between two contradictory beliefs: that my father's death was of no great importance, and that it damaged me forever.

I had nightmares almost every night. I especially disliked the one about being trapped, unable to escape, but I had it repeatedly. *The bus driver and I are the only ones left on the bus. As I get up to leave, I find I'm attached to the seat or the floor with a sticky substance. I start to free myself. First an arm, then a leg, and the other leg. Just as I'm about to escape, I get reattached and the process starts all over again.* It was hard to be attached to men who no longer existed, then to believe that either my mother was responsible or I was.

One day Henry and I went to the movies and there was a contest—the winner would spend a day with Gene Autry. The lady on the stage made the grand announcement: "808 is the winning number! Whoever has 808, please come up here!" Ticket number 808 wins a day with Gene Autry. My heart was pounding. I had a knack for numbers, and I remembered them very well. I couldn't believe it: I had the winning ticket, 808! I'd never won anything before. A day at the rodeo with Gene Autry—it seemed unimaginable. I'd never met a famous person. In fact, I had rarely left the five-block radius that surrounded my house. Now I would get a whole day of attention from a handsome man I had long admired. I was a little scared at the thought, but I was also thrilled. I started to search for my ticket. I was horrified! Where was it? I looked everywhere, but I couldn't find it. The woman on the stage announced, "If 808 doesn't come forward, we'll have to draw another number." But I have 808, I desperately told the usher. "Nothing I can do about it," he replied. Time passed. "808," she shouted again, and no one answered.

Later that day, when the movie was over and another winner had been selected, I was sitting on our stoop feeling forlorn, and I reached into my little paper lunch bag. My ticket stub—number 808—sat at the bottom. I wished I could run back and demand my day with Gene Autry, but I didn't even try. It was too late. I was thinking: Maybe it's for the best. I'm not so sure that someone as ordinary as me should be spending the day with a famous cowboy. What would I say to him? Maybe he would just ignore me. Maybe he would seat me in the stands and simply forget me there. But I couldn't rid myself of the image: me riding on a horse side by side with Gene Autry, just like on television. Why did I have to find that ticket now? Wouldn't it have been better if I had dropped it, or remembered the number incorrectly, instead of being a foolish kid who put her ticket stub in her lunch bag for safekeeping and then forgot all about it? I had my chance with an important man, and I lost it. The feeling was intolerable. I wished it had never happened. I wished I could escape. Is there any escape from feelings you don't want to have anymore, don't ever want to remember again?

As Mom got sicker, Sam's visits became the only carefree time we had together. Sam was more like a playmate than a father. He never got mad or ordered us around. On Saturday night, Mom and Sam would go to a nightclub. Mom had a beautiful photograph showing the two of them seated side by side at a fancy little table, smoking cigarettes and drinking liquor. Then, on Sunday, Sam would come back and take us out, to the Bronx Zoo or Palisades Amusement Park. The zoo was unimaginably big, and I loved the animals. For five cents, you could buy a slimy little fish, walk out onto a platform above the sea lion pool, and throw the seals their lunch. We could take the subway to the zoo, and sometimes I saved Mom money by sneaking under the turnstile, which seemed OK to do since I was just a little girl and hardly took up any room anyway.

I had a specific technique for visiting Palisades Amusement Park. First, I went on the merry-go-round and the roller coaster. Then an assortment of rides that whip you around and turn you upside down and spin you in circles. Then I got hungry, and Sam would buy me soda and cotton candy and anything else I wanted to eat. Then I would pick out one more ride, a good fast spinning one, become totally sick on it, get off, and throw up. Occasionally I contemplated skipping the last ride with its inevitable physiological consequences, but it was so tempting that vomiting seemed a small price to pay. One time I persuaded Alexis to go on the roller coaster with me, even though she was terrified of it. The ride started, Alexis began crying hysterically, and I screamed for the operator to stop. He didn't hear me, and even if he had, I'm sure he wouldn't have listened. I felt painfully guilty, waiting for the ride to end. Alexis remembered this betrayal for a long time. Once Sam won a goldfish for me by tossing a Ping-Pong ball right into the little glass jar containing the fish. I got to bring it home, and Sam was my hero.

At Christmas, I would tell Sam which doll I wanted, and he would deliver precisely the one I asked for. At Easter, he brought me a gigantic chocolate Easter bunny, with a bow tied around its neck, carrying a basket filled with jelly beans. The base of the bunny was solid chocolate, so it took almost a week to finish the whole thing. Sometimes before he came over, Sam would call and say he'd be passing the ice cream parlor, so what flavors did we want. Then we would wait eagerly until he walked in the door, bringing exactly what we had ordered.

When Sunday night came, I couldn't bear to see Sam leave. A whole week would pass before he would return. I grabbed his leg and made him drag me to the door before letting him go. Mom told me to stop, but when Sam was around I didn't listen very well.

Since I barely remembered my father, I struggled over what his loss meant to me through my relationships with every suitable substitute, and each played a role in my private battle over how to preserve or destroy his image. My love for Grandpa, Julius, and Sam seemed a continuation of the magical connection to the handsome father I had known, another chance to be the adorable little girl I once was in his eyes. And then, alternatively, when no man was around, I held on to my father by emulating his masculine behavior, being one of the guys, good at male pursuits, a hardy survivor who could protect Mom and be her most reliable companion. But sometimes I just couldn't forgive Dad for deserting me, and then I wished I could be rid of him altogether. So my competition with my unruly brother and my contempt for sadistic Uncle Hy and ineffectual Uncle Milton became a way of dismissing the usefulness of men completely. I didn't need what I didn't have. When this failed to console me, I stewed in my envy of all my classmates who had fathers, and when I got tired of doing that, I just felt sad.

I was only three when my father died, his influence on me unquestionably significant yet barely recorded in my memory. But losing my mother would be another matter entirely. The details of our life together were indelible in my mind. The longer I knew her, the more she served as my center, and I built my life and sense of self around my connection to her, the one person I knew, and loved, and remembered like no other. She was all I had left, irreplaceable, and it was impossible to think of going on without her.

Chapter 2

IMPOSSIBILITIES

(1 9 5 3 – 1 9 5 6)

Once I asked Mom what she had wanted to be when she
was little, and she told me a Spanish teacher, but she
had had to work during the day and go to college at night, and
her eyes were too bad to keep doing that, and it cost too much
money anyway. So she never finished. Mom was a secretary.
Her dresses were always getting torn on the left side from
reaching up to the switchboard she operated with her swollen
arm, but she did not complain. She went to work every day no
matter how she felt, except if she was in the hospital. Mom

and I took great comfort in behaving as though everything was as it should be.

"How can you play like that? Don't you realize your mother is in critical condition?" Alexis and I were chasing each other around the house, making plenty of noise. Mom was back in the hospital again, and her cousin was watching us for the afternoon. She was staring right at me, and her angry words stung me, angered me, reminded me of the unbridgeable gulf between myself and the adults around me. I knew nothing of what happened to Mom when she was in the hospital. No one talked to me about it. Mom didn't call, and children weren't allowed to visit. I didn't even understand what the word "critical" meant. Alexis wanted to know what it meant, too, and I realized I was the one responsible for explaining it to her. I went to the dictionary and looked it up, then looked up a word in the definition which I didn't understand, and then one I didn't know in that definition, and so on in a fruitless, whirling search for meaning. I realized my cousin wanted me to act like an adult, but it was too difficult to pretend I was grown-up all the time. Sometimes I just had to play. It was the only way I knew to stay calm in the face of danger.

There were times when I noticed more than most of the adults around me. Mom came home from work exhausted; she lay across the bed and started to cry. "Stop feeling sorry for yourself," Grandma admonished her. "Look at Larry. Now, he's someone to feel sorry for." Larry was the kid on our block who had only two little stubs where his arms should have been. Almost no one in the neighborhood wanted to play with him, so in defiance he would lunge at us, waving his stubs, laughing diabolically, powerful in his powerlessness. But I couldn't see what Larry's unhappiness had to do with Mom. I'd never seen Mom cry before, not that I could remember, nor heard her complain. Now finally she was offering a glimpse of what she felt inside. I wasn't sure what was more upsetting, Mom crying or Grandma attacking her for it. I was certainly sorry for her, and I wanted to comfort her. But watching them left me paralyzed with fright. Mom never cried in front of Grandma again, and for the first time it dawned on me that staying silent was Mom's safest choice.

When Mom came home from the hospital this time, she started to give herself injections. Standing alone in front of the full-length mirror in my tiny triangular bedroom, she would inject herself with her white medicine, splotches of it spraying the glass. I hated injections and couldn't imagine how Mom could stick herself like that. I never saw her do it, but in the early morning or late at night, when the house was quiet and I had my room to myself again, I stared at the patterns of splattered white liquid that Mom had left behind on my mirror, and I wondered what it really meant.

"Why do you breathe hard like that?" I asked her. Mom's breathing was getting more labored, and she was visibly short of breath now. "There's fluid around my lungs, and they use needles to take it out." I pictured a contraption that looked like an electric chair. They would strap her in tight and then turn the machine on. Two very long needles would slowly press forward, driven by a mechanical device, and puncture the skin of her back between her ribs on each side. The suction would begin and drain all that bad fluid. Then she'd be able to breathe.

———

That's not at all how it works, you know, but I wouldn't learn that until I was an intern at Montefiore Hospital in New York City. The patient is sitting hunched over on the edge of the bed. I've draped her back with white cloth and scrubbed the skin with Betadine to make it sterile. The pleural effusion on the X ray is only at the base of the right lung. We use a small needle and syringe to take a sample and test it for cancer cells. There's no machinery, no mechanical device, no one strapped into a chair. The process is quotidian, banal, utterly devoid of the drama with which my young imagination had imbued it.

Mom grew facial hair, and had to shave in the mornings like a man. "It's the injections," she told me. I didn't think someone as pretty as Mom wanted to have a beard, and I felt sorry for her. I worried about what it meant for a woman to start becoming like a man, and wondered why she had to take a medicine that would do this to her. Although I knew about death, I could not accept that Mom now faced it. I was hoping I didn't have to accept it, hoping that our silent pact protected both of us from the terror I perceived just past the horizon, the panic that our world was about to disintegrate. And I would never forget what it was like to cling to something that is no longer possible.

My new admission is a fifty-five-year-old woman with advanced ovarian cancer. She has come to the hospital before, but now we have run out of options. This time she has come here to die. Her husband is desperate and panicked, and cannot accept that his wife has reached the end. For days I try to

make him understand, and, failing, I mention all the counseling services we offer at the hospital. He is having none of it
because whatever else is true, his wife is not going to die. And
then she dies. Death, in its routine relentlessness, transforms
her body. In only minutes, her skin has yellowed and cooled,
and her muscles have stiffened. But the man is oblivious to
the changes that for most adults signal the irreversible movement from life to death. He throws himself onto the hospital
bed, hugging the pale body, refusing to let us take it to the
morgue. I gently insist. He turns, looking up at me like a cor-
nered animal. Now he's peering into the eyes of a doctor who
is shocked to see a grown man so undone, and simultaneously
overcome by the terror of being that little girl who watched
her own mother die. Then he bolts from the room, running. I
regain my composure. Wait for me! Don't run away! Let me
help you manage all that fear and panic! I run after him, I
shout, but I can't keep up. He runs out of the hospital, and
vanishes.

It was a stunning confrontation with denial of death, but I
myself would spend a lifetime alternately seeking and then
resisting the replacement of my own childlike fantasies with
an adult appraisal of all that had happened. How could the
disappearances of people so important to me be explained as
merely an arbitrary twist of fate? How could I be only a helpless spectator, passively watching while those around me
became ill and died? No child with even the slightest imagination could consider such a story credible. So I tried to make
sense of the world and, in the process, regain control. I
became convinced that any event, no matter how terrible,
could occur only under my personal influence, and that if I
behaved well enough, and stayed close enough, I could keep
my mother alive. I carefully monitored her, intervening when

she needed help, silently sympathizing with her physical struggles and her emotional pain, scolding myself whenever my own pleasures distracted me from my self-appointed task. If watching and worrying could have made a difference, my mother would have lived forever.

It was hard for me to tell the difference between a serious illness and a minor one, so everything made me nervous. Alexis had eczema, and when it was really bad, Mom had to soak the oozing sores on her arms and legs and then put all sorts of creams on them. Bandaged with yards and yards of white gauze, Alexis looked like a mummy. Then she had her tonsils out and she got to eat all the ice cream she wanted. I wished I could eat that much ice cream, but I was scared of operations, so I didn't wish too hard. And Alexis had more cavities than teeth. The school dentist found thirty-two cavities when she went for her first checkup in kindergarten!

Bad teeth ran in our family, and one day Mom had to take me to the dental clinic to have four rotten baby teeth extracted. It all took place under anesthesia, but when I woke up, my mouth was full of blood, like Grandpa's stomach was right before he died, so I started screaming at the top of my lungs. "Mother, get this child out of here," the dentist shouted. Dentists, especially the ones who worked in the clinic, were very mean.

I had astigmatism, which they told me meant my eyes were uneven, although they looked perfectly even to me. I had a little game I played with my eyes when I lay in bed at night. I would press them with my fingers until I saw designs, like the geometric patterns on the rug in the movie theater, and I felt like I was floating, suspended in air, looking down at the floor below. I wondered now if this had caused my problem, but I found the sensation comforting, so I continued to do it anyway. During an eye examination, they gave me eyedrops, and then I looked through different lenses to see which worked best. That night, when I was lying in bed, I saw something weird: pillows were under my dresser, and they kept marching over to my bed. Marching pillows were not particularly scary—not at all like a bad dream—but I had to keep getting out of bed to chase them back, and I hardly got any sleep. Not until medical school would I realize what had happened: atropine eyedrops, used to dilate the eyes, can cause visual hallucinations.

My knee played tricks on me, too. I'd be walking along on a class trip, and suddenly my knee would lock up and I wouldn't be able to walk. "Wait for me!" I shouted as the entire class moved through a corridor of the UN building, and I feared I'd be left behind. Mom took me for X rays, and I listened while she and the doctor discussed the problem. But since I didn't understand a word they were saying, I stared, fascinated, at the picture of my bones, delighted by the little gray metal numbers they put near my knee which now showed up looking so white on the X ray. And the doctor was right when he said it would go away by itself. Another mystery solved in medical school: this is called a joint mouse. A piece of bone breaks off and floats in the synovial fluid that fills the joint, sometimes positioning itself in a way that prevents the joint from moving. Eventually, the bone is resorbed and the problem disappears.

You had to get to the medical clinic early in the morning because the wait was long. You got a green plastic disk with a number on it and then sat, interminably, on hard wooden benches. Playing with the plastic disk, bored nearly to tears, I noticed that there was a little hole at the top, perfect for sticking my finger in. But then I couldn't get it out! I was stuck! They're going to cut my finger off to get it out! That's what doctors do when there's trouble with body parts! Mom told me to calm down: we'd go to the bathroom and put soap and water on it to make it slip off. It'll never work! My finger is finished! Yet in the bathroom, in a few seconds, off it came. To my great relief, my finger would remain attached.

I was nine and I felt tiny lumps under my nipples. I was ashamed to admit that I was frightened by them, but I didn't think they belonged there, and I wondered if something terrible was happening to my body. I waited until we saw Dr. Sonberg, and I got up the courage to show him. Oh, you're just growing up, he told me, and I was reassured when I realized he meant that I was only getting ordinary breasts.

If I got sick and had to stay home from school, Mom went to work anyway. She had to, because we needed the money. Even so, Mom would buy me the expensive liquid penicillin in chocolate syrup instead of making me take the ground-up bitter white pills. Before she left, she would measure the medicine into little whiskey glasses and leave me notes with the exact time to swallow each portion, plus sour-ball candies and little glass dishes filled with pretty-colored Jell-O to eat all day long. Then she would call me during the day, or I'd call her. I felt brave, and grown-up, a responsible person my mother trusted to stay home all alone and take care of herself. Once my brother and I got sick together—whooping cough. We were standing in the kitchen, vomiting all over the place, and it was just too much. So Mom had to stay home that time. Often I worried that we were just a burden to her, and when

she was gone I would convince myself that our demands had
drained what little life was left in her, that death was her
escape from having to care for us.

Sometimes Mom got so sick she had to suddenly go to the hospital. Various relatives would come to help take care of us. On
one occasion, when no one was able to come, Mom hired
someone to live with us. That was the best solution so far, I
thought, because this was the nicest and most patient person
I'd ever met, and she wasn't one bit mad at us about our mother being sick. I had the impression that she even felt sorry for
us, which seemed odd to me, and I was a little embarrassed by
her sentiments, sweet and unfamiliar.

When Mom got home, I tried to be extra good. One time she
came back with presents for each of us. I got a little hat made of
felt. "But I want the hat," Alexis insisted, and she started to cry.
I took her aside. "Don't upset Mom. She made these presents
while she was very sick in the hospital, so we have to act happy
to get them." Alexis was still upset, but then she fell in love
with the doggie Mom made for her, and pulled it all around
the house by a string, having decided that it was much better
than a boring old hat anyway. I didn't like to show disappointment if I didn't like what Mom got me. I knew where she
kept our birthday presents, so sometimes I would sneak a look
at mine in advance. Then, if it wasn't what I wanted, I could
feel my disappointment in private and act enthusiastic when
she gave it to me. I felt a little guilty about sneaking around
and pretending, but I had to be very careful not to make Mom
any sicker than she already was.

But it was good that I had so much to do to help Mom stay
well. I liked to be useful. Of course, I could drive her crazy,

too. She would ask me to go to the grocery store to buy, say, butter, eggs, American cheese, and Ritz crackers. Instead of making a list, I would make up a word using the first letter of each item. I liked to play these mental games, because while I was doing it, I didn't have to think much about anything else. So I memorized the word "bear," and Mom gave me the money. All the way down to the store I repeated the word— "b-e-a-r, butter, eggs, American cheese, Ritz crackers"—and when I got to the store I recited the items to the man behind the counter. With long lists, the game became more intricate. I had to add letters at the end of real words, or make up words that didn't even exist: How else could you get two j's— jelly and juice—into the same word? Mom kept insisting I should write it down, but I always argued that I didn't really need to, and I could see that my stubborn refusal was driving her nuts. But I had to do it this way because otherwise it wouldn't have been any fun. For the most part, though, I tried not to annoy her. I volunteered to fold the laundry. I watched Alexis when Mom was busy. I did whatever I thought she wanted done, and I was careful not to offend.

I monitored Mom's emotions as closely as I did her physical health, sometimes feeling them so intensely that it was difficult to remember my own. Her anger devastated me. She bought me a blue-and-white-checkered wool jacket, flared at the bottom, pretty and feminine. I had begged her for it, even though it was much too expensive. The first day I wore it, I was playing after school. I got hot, took off the jacket, and left it on a rock, forgetting all about it. Mom yelled at me furiously when I arrived home without it. How could I lose my jacket the very first day after she'd spent all that money on it? I listened, and as her face flushed with rage I could feel her exhaustion and frustration and despair. What I had done was indefensible, so I offered no defense. I wished I could reverse it, which I tried to do in a hopeless search for the jacket the next day. There was no money for another one, and I began to feel sorry for myself, too, because I had lost my beautiful jacket and would never be able to wear it again.

Losing that jacket became attached in my mind to losing my mother. Our moments of pleasure were growing further and further apart, and now we rarely laughed or played together. In her dying, she was slipping away from me, and I could not bear to let her go. I pursued her, sharing her painful feelings as a way to stay close. Eventually, my preoccupation with her suffering defined my attachment to her, and apart from it I had little sense of myself. Losing track of Mom's struggles became synonymous with letting her disappear, body and spirit, for I did not yet understand that my internal relationship to her was everlasting.

In the summer when I was at camp, I could sometimes stop dwelling on my mother's illness. But then, by the time I returned, something new had gone wrong. "You can hug me," she said when I got home the summer I was eight. But I was still hesitant. She looked so fragile with that bandage around her head. I was afraid I would hurt her. I was also upset and surprised. None of her letters to camp mentioned that she had been in the hospital or had had surgery. It horrified me to think that while I was away having a good time, she was at home getting sicker. The next summer, I found the bandages on her stomach; it was a shock to come home and find her changed yet again. And later on, whenever I was separated from those I loved, I'd always wonder whether they might in my absence undergo some disturbing physical transformation.

The sicker Mom got, the more she lived on the edge, tense, irritable—and increasingly her perfect control was punctured.

"You're killing me," she shouted. Her neck veins bulged. I thought they might burst and she'd die right then and there. But when nothing happened, I concluded that it was Mom's way of saying this was all entirely too much for her. I instantly regretted any offense I may have committed, and even the ones I hadn't committed. It didn't make sense to defend myself—I was on her side, with her in her impossible struggle. But daily life continued much the same as always. She cleaned the house, made our lunches, looked after us. Who could believe there would be a final day?

A huge construction project was under way in our neighborhood: the building of the Cross Bronx Expressway. Adults were constantly talking about this—why, I couldn't imagine, since to me there seemed no subject more excruciatingly boring than road building. They said the road would go right through our own apartment house, chatter which seemed to me not only dull but preposterous—why would they pick our house to build a road through when there were so many other houses around? Yet, incredibly, my house was in the way, so they tore it down. We moved to another apartment two blocks away.

Our new apartment was smaller and run-down, but Sam came over to fix it up, applying all his skills as a painter and plasterer. I still liked to dance for Sam, but now Mom told me to put on more clothes because I was too big to continue parading around in gossamer scarves. One day I came home from school and I accidentally walked in on Sam, who had just finished painting one of the bedrooms and was now changing out of his paint-splattered work clothes. Naked from the waist down, he fixed me with a stare that was so intense

and so piercing that it remained with me forever, indelible. It
dawned on me that while Mom had only one breast and the
beginnings of a beard, I was becoming a woman with two
breasts. I was horrified by the contrast, and it marked the
moment when competing with Mom for Sam's attention was
no longer any fun. My childish wish to be the prettier one simply folded into the long nightmare in which Mom deteriorat-
ed while I grew and survived.

Mom had bought a pale pink couch so the new apartment
would look prettier. She was in the hospital the day it arrived.
"Don't sit on it," Grandma instructed me, and then explained
that poor sick Mom had been struggling to save her money so
she could finally buy something really nice for the house, and
we had to wait until she came home from the hospital and let
her be the first one to try it out. But after Grandma left the
room, the pink couch was still there, lustrous and irresistible.
I gave in to my impulse, jumping up and landing backward on
the taut cushions, and it was nice and bouncy just like I'd
hoped. But then the terror came to hover: what would follow
from my transgression? Everyone knows: "Step on a crack,
break your mother's back!"

After this hospitalization, Mom decided she was too ill to
care for Henry. He was twelve when she sent him to someplace called the Pleasantville Cottage School. It was the
spring before Mom died when Alexis and I first visited Henry
there, and I'd never seen so many flowers all lined up in rows,
beautiful, purple and sweet-smelling. "When lilacs last in the
dooryard bloomed" comes to mind every time, as an adult, I
think of the place. I wasn't sure why Henry was living here, or
whom this place was for. And despite its pretty name and
bucolic appearance, and the nameless "cottage parents" Henry
referred to, I suspected this was a place for bad children, ban-

ished and punished. I was thankful I was only visiting, and prayed to God, even though He didn't really exist, to save me from a fate like this. I refused to think of Mom as the one from whom God would have to save me. If I did that, how could I depend on her?

April 5 was Mom's birthday. I always bought her nylons because that was the only thing she ever wanted. She didn't like impractical gifts. She would have bought the nylons for herself anyway, so it didn't seem like much of a present. But saving up my allowance, buying them, wrapping them in pretty paper, presenting them to Mom at the right moment on the right day all this was more important than the nylons themselves. On Sundays, if we went to the ice cream parlor, we would walk back past a store window with beautiful little dolls in taffeta dresses. I longed for one, but Mom said no, and then, when I insisted, she stared impassively and said not one more word. I especially admired the doll with the green dress with white lacy edges. I decided to save my allowance every week, and then, after several months, in some peculiar twist of childish logic, I determined that if she couldn't buy the doll for me, I would buy it for her.

Just before her forty-eighth birthday, the last she would celebrate, Mom came out of the hospital yet again. This time, instead of boring nylons, I had a pretty doll for her. I covered it in wrapping paper, counted down the days until April 5 arrived, and then gave it to her. When she unwrapped it and saw I had defied her and wasted her money on something so utterly useless, she became furious. "You'll be sorry when I'm dead!" she shouted as she collapsed on the couch, that pink couch where fear now seemed to linger permanently. This was the first and only time she threatened so directly to leave me. The thought filled me with dread.

I walked back to the couch, knelt next to her, and pleaded, "Please don't die." She was silent, self-contained again, back in control, now recognizably my normal mother. I imagined that she was more upset with herself for getting so angry than with me for buying the doll. I am sorry I said that, her silence implied, I'm at my wit's end, I'm sick and getting sicker, I have no reassurance to offer, and I am exhausted. I felt her unspoken forgiveness, and I was sorry for both of us. Still, I used her outburst as part of the evidence against me. My mother was dying not because some horrible disease had invaded her lungs to suffocate her, but because I was bad.

I am not far along in my psychiatric training when I am assigned to treat a thirty-seven-year-old woman with two children, an eleven-year-old daughter whom she has brought along to the interview, and a seven-year-old son who is in the hospital dying of a brain tumor. Mother and daughter select seats far apart, and the little girl sits in silence, cowering. The mother begins to explain her situation, and soon she is shouting and crying, angrily accusing her daughter of being her bad child while offering a pained and frightening description of the boy she labels her good one. Her son was once an adorable Little Leaguer; now he is a bald invalid who can barely walk. The mother leaps from her chair. "Look at her," she screams, pointing to her daughter, her feelings of hatred and desperation now overwhelming her. "It should have been her!"

My patient has no control over herself, I have no control over the interview, and the little girl is completely helpless. I recollect my mother's momentary fury over the little doll with the taffeta dress—a glimpse into the world of unremitting rage and desperation she shared with Henry. I liked to think I was

Mom's favorite—I wasn't intentionally provocative, like Henry, and I wasn't little and needy with weeping skin, like Alexis. But if I was the least trouble, then wasn't I at the same time the least visible, hiding out where I could be reached by neither Mom's rage nor her love? I could not resolve the paradox.

Mom and I went on pretending everything was normal, no matter what changed around us, and no matter how sick she got. I went on believing my mother couldn't disappear, that that could never happen. And I believed it couldn't happen because it would have been impossible for me to go on without her. Just as I had the previous summer, I was spending three weeks at camp. She sent these two postcards to me.

July 6, 1956
I hope you are feeling fine and having an enjoyable time. We are all well. How do you like the girls in your bunk and your counselors?

July 11, 1956
I have three of your Weekly Readers. Do you want me to hold them for you or shall I mail them to you? I don't suppose you have too much time for reading with all those activities going on. Lots of love and kisses xxxxxxxxxx from all of us. Mom

On August 29, Mom died.

Chapter 3

ORPHAN

(1956)

The mirrors were covered with sheets when I arrived home from my Aunt Anne's house. Mom was nowhere to be found. Something was wrong. The adults were huddled in the kitchen, and they were ignoring me. I demanded to be included, questioning them persistently. Finally, Aunt Milly left the table and took me to my room. What's happening? I pleaded. Aunt Milly and I were sitting side by side on the bed in my little cluttered room, both of us staring straight ahead. Still she remained silent.

I was twenty-four years old, in my third year of medical school, before I finally had the words to explain exactly how my mother died. There was something comforting about bringing that part of my childhood confusion to a close. The mastectomy had left Mom's arm swollen from the removal of the lymph nodes, a condition known as lymphedema. But the cancer had spread further. The bandage on her head followed a hypophysectomy, the severing of the pituitary gland to interfere with hormonal support for the growth of the cancer cells. The abdominal bandage covered the wound from an oophorectomy, the removal of the ovaries, to further reduce estrogen stimulation. The beard must have been caused by injections of male hormones, used to get the metastatic cancer cells to regress. The final event: diffuse metastatic disease of the lungs. She suffocated.

"Your mother is in heaven," my Aunt Milly finally offered. Until that moment, I had been holding on tight: Mom was still alive until someone in authority declared otherwise. But since I was almost sure she was dead, the tension of self-deception quickly became unbearable. Twice before the mirrors in our house had been covered, once for Dad and once for Grandpa. I knew what this meant, yet simultaneously it felt like I didn't know, and I clung to the frail hope that the unacceptable had not happened. When no one was looking, I lifted one of the sheets and sneaked a look at my own reflection, recalling the forbidden bounce on the new pink couch, defying death by refusing to comply with the rituals that surrounded it. But Milly's words now were undeniable, her manner unmistakable. I had been hurled over the cliff. The irreversibility of what had happened crashed down on me; a nauseating wave of fear and a flood of tears followed. I didn't know who I was without my mother. For the past six years my life had revolved around watching the inexorable deterioration of her health, monitoring her downward course, trying to figure out how to improve things, however slightly. Yet the essence of my mother remained to the very end in her toughness, her determination, her consistently conscientious ministrations. The example she set of how to fight in the face of adversity would become the most important gift she bequeathed to me. What would fill the vast space left by the disappearance of this all-consuming relationship? How would I spend my time? What would I become?

When I began practicing medicine, I learned to sense what patients wanted me to discuss with them, and what they'd rather not hear. With each encounter of this kind, I reflected on my own history. Did my mother's strategy—carefully shielding us from confronting her deteriorating state—spare us, or did she merely leave us ill equipped to deal with a future that she must have known would be painful? If asked, most mental health professionals would say that denial is something to be overcome. The best approach is to face one's problems, to put what's happening into words. But we acted as if we'd fall apart if we were realistic. In medical school, I read a study demonstrating that people who deal with their heart attacks by using denial are more likely to survive than those who face the issue squarely and worry about their disease. I looked for this kind of evidence that denial is good, trying to make sense of why we were desperate to maintain it. But when I actually saw how powerful denial could be, when, looking from the outside, I saw it in action, I felt only the underlying terror.

"Remember when you came into the hospital and you needed all those blood transfusions?" I am speaking to a gray-haired sixty-one-year-old bachelor, likable and somewhat eccentric. He looks at me, completely uncomprehending, and my own anxiety intensifies. My patient has had three pints of blood since his admission only five days ago. He is perfectly intelligent and lucid. I can see he is frightened, but when he can't even acknowledge the blood transfusions, how can I tell him that the reason he is bleeding is that he has esophageal cancer? I know this will be a difficult discussion, so I have set aside an hour for it. I am determined to master this, to learn how to talk to scared people about cancer, to learn not to be so scared myself. But now I wonder if even this will be enough time to get through to him. I sneak up on the subject, forty-five minutes of conversation. Yes, he finally concedes, maybe he did receive some blood, and he does remember that they put a tube down his throat to look for the cause of his bleeding, and that they took a biopsy. Good. Now for the bad news: We've found a tumor, I tell him. Silence. I wait, hoping he will ask the question. I hold my breath, recalling my own struggle between knowing and not knowing. Is it cancer? he finally asks. I feel relieved. Yes, I tell him, but we caught it very early. We'd like you to have surgery. There's a good chance for a cure. I don't say how rare a cure is, even though the surgeon has assured me that this man is one of the few patients he's seen with a really good chance, and I don't mention what a terrible disease esophageal cancer is if it isn't cured. I want him to hear my simple message and take my advice, but he can do neither. The next morning, he signs out of the hospital and goes home. I feel defeated.

"So you're Dr. Cournos," a young woman I do not know says to me, reading my ID badge as we ride down in the hospital elevator together. Yes, I answer, perplexed. "You treated my uncle three months ago. You told him he had esophageal cancer. He signed out and went to another hospital a week later. He told them he had cancer and needed an operation. I'm a social worker here, and I was wondering who you were." I am astonished to get this follow-up on a patient I thought had disappeared permanently.

"How's he doing?"

"He had the surgery, and he feels fine."

I am delighted, amazed. He did hear me, even if he couldn't admit he had. Maybe telling him such bad news made him angry. Maybe it would have been humiliating to accept surgery from the very people who had so aggrieved him by telling him he had cancer. Maybe he just didn't trust us. Or maybe I had overwhelmed him with my diagnosis of espohageal cancer just as I had been overwhelmed by Aunt Milly's announcement of my mother's death. But at least for my patient I had words of hope; I was relieved to learn that he had heard them.

For one week our house was packed with people sitting shiva, the traditional seven days of mourning. Just about everyone we knew showed up (except my banished brother Henry), as well as many people I'd never even seen before. The house was bustling—lots of food, plenty of small talk, even a degree of merriment. I was bored and horrified at once: Didn't these people understand that the world had been transformed in some unimaginably horrible way? Silently, I leveled the same charge at them as my Mom's cousin once had at me. How can you be playing when my mother has died?

Sixth grade had just started, and I was huddled with my five classmates on a street corner, catching up from our summer break. I was ashamed to tell them, but I finally got up the courage. My mother died. One week ago. That's all I said. My friends looked ill at ease, shifting from one foot to another, saying nothing. I felt bad for them. Well, at least I had gotten it over with. Still, I was left thinking: Would they now think less of me? Children without parents are bad: they lost them—killed them—drove them away. I hated myself— hated my body—hated how I looked. My yellow polo shirt clung to my body, revealing my tiny breasts. Shame on me for letting them show. I folded my arms across my chest to hide them.

The mourning period passed. Now no one came to our house. The refrigerator was filled with boxes and boxes of chocolates that our guests had left behind. Although chocolate was my favorite food—or rather because chocolate was my favorite food—I was trying not to eat it, to avoid getting pleasure from something that seemed a consequence of my mother's death. I thought of the warm comfort of eating those chocolates the policemen had given me when I was lost in Crotona Park, and I had never felt more lost than I felt now. As my loneliness mounted, so did my craving. I couldn't stand it anymore, and the first bite of one piece unleashed a voracious desire to consume it all. I devoured them by the handful, a starving person who had found the only food in the world, box after box over the following days, until not a single chocolate was left.

A psychoanalyst might see my behavior as an attempt to avoid an inner emptiness by filling up on food. Some psychiatric researchers say chocolate contains a chemical that makes it an antidepressant. I don't think a day has passed since the chocolate orgy that followed my mother's death when I haven't eaten something chocolate, and whatever the psychological or physiological facts may be, they matter little to me.

"Where's Mom?" my little sister asked. Weeks had passed since her death. Despite all the talk in our house, no one had informed Alexis, and she had not figured it out. Our mother had ceased to exist, but this apparently required no explanation. We did not say goodbye to her at the funeral. We were not invited. Eventually, experts in death and dying would make clear how important it is to include children in mourning rituals, but when I was a little girl, there was no professional guidance for this sort of thing. We had to depend on common sense, a commodity in short supply.

"Who will tell Alexis?" I had asked my Aunt Milly the day she told me Mom died. She had answered with silence. And so I waited.

"I'll do it," I finally announced. I'd better do it sometime soon. Alexis was seven years old and four grades behind me, but I was afraid she'd hear about it from one of my classmates.

"Have you heard of heaven?" I asked, paraphrasing Milly's words to me, but not connecting them in any way to Mom's death. I'd selected a strategy, one I'd learned well: I would spare my sister from suffering. I described the pleasure of life in heaven after death, explaining how much better things are in the next world. It didn't matter that I didn't believe in the next world. I'd been raised without formal religion, but there was no escaping being Jewish, no matter how little attention I had given to Judaism. Besides, my grandmother had told me all about the goyim and the evils of Christianity. She needn't have bothered. I wasn't interested in anybody's God. I didn't believe He existed. And if He does exist, He stinks. He took my parents away. What good is He anyway? I hated all that "It's-God's-will-and-it-works-out-for-the-best-in-God's-own-way" stuff.

But for the purposes of my task, heaven was just fine. And, I informed my sister, if Mom were to die, she would go to this wonderful place where she would be much happier than she was here on earth and where she could watch over us at every moment. As I said it, I realized that I sort of believed in that part a little, or at least I wanted to—that my mom still knew what I was doing even if she couldn't be here, that she could see I was still her reliable helper, and that I was slowly getting up my courage to tell Alexis.

Because it seemed the most appropriate location for them, we usually had our private conversations in the bathroom. A comfortable, intimate room, good for sharing secrets. White walls, white tiles, no distractions from the task at hand. One of us would sit on the lowered toilet seat, the other on the edge of the tub. Maybe we believed we wouldn't be disturbed here, although the only other person in the house was Grandma, and she seemed largely oblivious to what we did. Anyway, I'd stopped using the bathroom to brush my teeth, since it didn't cross my mind to do it, and almost stopped using it to bathe and wash my hair, which I remembered to do every two weeks or so, which seemed often enough.

The bathroom was also the place for my hysterical fit every morning when, staring unhappily at my thin, pointy-chinned face in the mirror, I tried to comb my long brown hair into a perfect ponytail, with every hair in place. I would scream because I had to do it over and over again. Grandma would come in to see what was wrong. Go away! No one can help me! Finally, I got it just so, no hairs sticking up in ugly bumps. I needed to feel control over something.

At last the moment arrived to tell Alexis the truth—or at least half of it. Mom has died, I told my sister, and she has gone to heaven. I was sitting on the rim of the bathtub. It worked! My sister greeted the news with a mixture of mild puzzlement and good cheer. She knew Mom was happy, and invisibly watching over us.

Over the years, as I grew up, I realized that my mother's death gave me responsibilities toward my sister that I was ill prepared to carry out. My inadequate explanation left her with the legacy of having the wrong initial response to her own mother's death—feeling obliged to act as if this was in some sense good news. In later years, convinced that I had profoundly harmed her, terrible feelings of guilt came over me, unmitigated by the knowledge that I too was a child in need of care. However understandably, I was a poor substitute parent, a failure at the job, and to this day it remains a source of discomfort between my sister and me. I thought I was protecting her, but I could not comprehend or even foresee the inevitability of the pain we would both have to experience. I have often had to tell people that someone they love has died. Even so, it is not easy. I was eleven years old the first time I did it. I think I have become better at it since then.

When I am an attending psychiatrist at Columbia, I'll learn that even an expert can run away from the magnitude of a child's pain. I'm sitting through a lecture given by a psychoanalyst on the subject of Edward Weston, whose mother died when he was five. The lecturer explains how those exquisite feminine photographs of such objects as peppers revealed Weston's anxiety about his mother's castration. I wait for the talk to end. At the end of the discussion period, I have the last question. "Why would Weston be worried about his mother's missing penis, which never even existed, when he was missing his entire mother, which he once had and then lost?" He restates his theories, never answering my question. All the while I am thinking he just finds it too difficult to comprehend the magnitude of losing an entire mother. Much better to concentrate on some imaginary part. Losing my parents, it seems to me, was losing a real part of myself, permanently.

Chapter 4

GRANDMA

(1956–1958)

After Mom died, we lived like three children—my grandmother, my sister, and me. At seventy-six, this was the first time my grandmother had ever been on her own, having married at seventeen and lived with another responsible adult ever since. Grandma had never worked or been to school. Although she understood English, she spoke only Yiddish, and I was proud to translate for her on our excursions into the South Bronx. Grandma tended to repeat herself, and her stories and rituals became part of the comfortable customs

of daily life, the link to the past, the center of whatever continuity and structure we still had.

We floated through the days, each in our own orbit, until
evening came, when our other activities were all done and we
could perform the nightly ritual of weeping over Mom's death.
Grandma would put her arms around each of us in turn, rocking back and forth in a bear hug. I felt her warm, full body
against mine, and we cried and cried. How could a daughter
die before her own mother? she would moan. While this was
the essence of the tragedy from Grandma's perspective, I was
busy feeling sorry for myself. Then she would look at us and
announce: "It's as if you were born from my own body." I
silently rejected Grandma's sentiment, since I wanted my real
mother back and would never agree that any substitute could
take her place.

Months went by, but our crying continued unabated. Then,
when Grandma was mad at us one night, she ended our routine with a nasty twist: "If your mother hadn't been so busy
taking care of you," she said, "she could have gone to the doctor in time and she wouldn't have died." I was horrified to discover that Grandma blamed us for Mom's death. For an
instant I stopped experiencing Grandma as a helpless companion and saw her as a witch. When we were adults, my
cousin Marlene, Anne's only daughter, described our grandmother: "She was the incarnation of selfishness and evil, the
source of all her children's impairments." But I was depending
on Grandma; I had to see her in the best possible light.

I missed my mother terribly; my life had lost its center.
There were particular moments: sometimes when there was a
special assembly at school and our class was standing on the
stage, all the girls dressed in white blouses with red scarves,

singing, I had to remind myself, Don't be looking around for a proud parent who has come to see you perform. If I didn't try, I didn't have to be disappointed.

I took comfort in what remained of the familiar, but even that kept changing. My neighborhood was falling apart. People had given up using garbage pails. Instead, they opened their windows and threw the garbage right into the courtyard of our building. Every day the pile grew higher. Some of our neighbors kept live roosters under the sidewalk gratings. I thought they were cute; Grandma said they were dirty. There was violence everywhere: even my school was now manned by police at every entrance and exit. One night from my apartment window I saw a man lying dead on the sidewalk in a pool of blood. He had been shot coming out of the candy store I visited regularly. While walking to school one day, I came across two men with knives, fighting. I sidestepped them and continued on my way. I was playing in the park when a teenage boy threatened to unleash his panting Doberman on my sister and me. I talked him down. Most of my friends were leaving for safer places—both Sarah and Rita would soon be moving to Queens—but for us it was a struggle just to stay in place. We were not going anywhere, but I didn't mind: my neighborhood reminded me of the life we had with Mom.

And it wasn't all bad, of course. On my new block there was a street vendor I'd never seen before, a short, round man who pushed a little cart calling "Jelly apples! Jelly apples!" I could hear him from our apartment. "Grandma, can I have five cents?" Then, if she had the money for me, I would run down for my apple. On the front of the cart was a huge stack of apples, and at the back a boiling pot of red jelly. I got to pick my own apple, and the man would put a stick in it. Then he would dip it into the boiling pot and lift it out, dripping and steaming, rotating it smoothly to catch every drop. The jelly immediately started to harden, and I would wait until the consistency was just right, not too hard, not too soft, before I took the first delicious bite.

Then there were the new immigrants who kept moving in, with their lively Latin music and their colorful clothing. A gigantic store opened on Bathgate Avenue with piles and piles of the most beautiful clothing I had ever seen. I bought a pair of black pants with embroidered white flowers for only three dollars, and a lovely yellow cotton skirt with big orange roses on it for even less. These were my favorite clothes. But most of the kids in our school didn't speak English, and it was boring to hear teachers talking about stuff I had learned long ago.

Grandma had only two skills my sister and I lacked: she knew how to clean, and she knew how to cook. The cleaning I didn't care about, but I loved her cooking. My favorite dish was kreplach, the Jewish version of meat-filled dumplings. Making them was a two-day process, complex and wonderful. First, we had to go to the poultry store on Bathgate Avenue to pick out a chicken. Grandma pointed to the one she wanted among all the chickens, which looked exactly the same to me. The butcher would grab the poor unfortunate chosen chicken, holding it against his stained white apron as he carried it cackling into the back room, where, mercifully out of sight of the customers, he beheaded it. If we were feeling rich, we paid extra to have him pluck the feathers out. If not, Grandma did it herself at home. The rest of Day One was consumed in chopping up vegetables, adding spices, and boiling them with the chicken for hours and hours in a giant pot. Day Two began with cutting up the chicken and combining it with various ingredients that transformed the mixture into a thick, brown tasty filling for the kreplach. Then came the best part: making a giant wad of dough, then rolling it out until it was thin and perfectly flat. I imitated Grandma, sprinkling flour on the heavy wooden rolling pin and pressing it down with all my might on the dough that rested on the wooden board. Finally—this was my specialty and the most aesthetically demanding step—we cut the dough into perfect squares, took exactly the right amount of filling, placed it in the center of the square, and sculpted the dough so it closed around the filling, two crisscrossed seams at the top and a nice round shape underneath. Into the chicken broth they went, boiled until they were tender and hot, and then served in the chicken soup: wonderful, juicy, plump dumplings whose flavor I would never forget. This was the most complicated task Grandma could handle. For almost everything else, we were on our own.

I liked to cook, too, but nothing as fancy as kreplach. My favorite dish I called Cheese Delight, which I made by melting a piece of American cheese on a slice of white toast. Then I would cut it into twelve perfectly symmetrical pieces and pull them apart so that Alexis and I each got six. Years later, Alexis was shocked to discover that you can get a grilled cheese sandwich at any diner. She firmly believed I had invented it.

Grandma liked to sit in the kitchen, her elbows perched on the linoleum cloth covering the table, and listen to the radio, positioning her head right next to it as if she feared that the sound could only travel a few inches before being lost forever. She especially liked a show called "The Romance of Helen Trent." There were apparently an endless number of episodes, and each began with a deep, echoing man's voice intoning "Can a woman over thirty-five still find true love?" Thirty-five was so old, it seemed to me, why would anyone worry about true love then? Scary things kept happening to Miss Trent, and although I hardly ever paid enough attention to follow the plot, I got the impression that her quest was pretty hopeless. On the other hand, the three of us were managing and we didn't have a man, so what was her problem? Besides, I kept thinking, if she ever actually does find true love, the show will have to end and Grandma will have nothing left to listen to.

Grandma had special cures for things, like the disgusting white goo she put on slices of raw potatoes to kill cockroaches. For heat rash, it was cornstarch; for mosquito bites, calamine lotion. And then, most impressive of all, there was the head-lice remedy. One morning I walked into Alexis's room and I was stunned: her hair and her pillow were covered with hundreds of tiny crawling insects, as if all the baby bugs had been born at the same time. The place was swarming with them. I raced to get Grandma, who was as astonished as I was. "Head lice," she proclaimed, and rummaged through the closet, eventually coming up with a can of kerosene—one of those nervous-making containers with a skull and crossbones printed on them. With this, she planned to shampoo my sister. We would do it in the bathroom, not in the kitchen, which Grandma explained was too close to the gas pilot light, which might cause the kerosene to ignite.

I knew all about fires. There were lots of them in my neighborhood. The most spectacular we ever saw was a five-story apartment building engulfed in flames, top to bottom, and when it was over, nothing was left of the building at all. Then we heard on the radio that six firemen had died, and everyone in the neighborhood was very sad. One day Grandma was lighting the oven and she forgot what she was doing, and left the gas on too long before striking the match. Then the whole stove went up in flames, just for a second, but long enough to burn Grandma's eyelashes off! It was scary at first, but then, when we realized she wasn't hurt, we laughed about how she looked walking around with no eyelashes. Despite our helplessness without Mom, things worked out, one way or another.

Although I didn't do much of a job with personal hygiene, I did manage to get to school every day, continue to get A's, keep watch over my sister, and—this really made me proud— learn to operate my grandmother's foot-pedal sewing machine. This required the perfect touch, to keep the needle moving smoothly so it wouldn't suddenly stop and tear the thread—a disaster, because it meant rethreading the machine before you could go on sewing, passing the thread through a series of loops and eyelets in exactly the right order, knowing that one wrong twist would make the thread break as soon as the machine started, and that the tiresome process would have to begin all over again.

When I was sick, Grandma would sometimes call Dr. Sonberg, but he charged seven dollars to come to our house, which Grandma said was way too much. So usually we walked to the clinic four blocks away, which only charged one dollar. Grandma let me do all the talking, even to the cashier. All things considered, it seemed to me, we were managing pretty well.

Grandma's favorite topic was herself. Usually we started with her birth in Poland. She was the youngest and most beautiful of her mother's eight children, the only one with blond hair and blue eyes. She was so beautiful that her mother had to keep constant watch over her to protect her from the evil eye of others' envy. People even offered to buy her, she told us, proposals that, of course, her mother always refused.

We were sitting on a wooden bench in Crotona Park on a beautiful sunny day, and I was trying to imagine Grandma young and beautiful. Grandma was soft and floppy now. Her face was completely wrinkled, and her earlobes sagged from years of wearing fancy heavy earrings. My favorites were the silver ones, shaped like harps, with little colored stones on them. "Do your ears hang low, do they wobble to and fro . . ." I liked that song and Grandma's wobbly ears. Loose skin hung from her upper arms and Alexis and I loved to touch it and make it jiggle. Grandma had two breasts, like me. Not just one, like Mom. And when she took off her brassiere and corset with all the white struts shaped like popsicle sticks (which Grandma said were whalebones!), then you could see them hang against her chest like two long, flat pancakes, reaching down to her waist. Her blue eyes had not changed, nor the waves in her short, thick hair, even though it was white now. It was spring, and the park looked pretty, and, yes, I could imagine Grandma as a baby, all blond and beautiful, her own mother pushing her along in a carriage.

Grandma interrupted my musings: "Always remember," she said, "marry a man who loves you more than you love him." Although I was doubtful about Grandma's advice, I never asked her to explain, and since anyway we had no man at all, I decided it was best just to take comfort in the predictability of Grandma's favorite utterances.

I got my period when I was twelve. The bleeding scared me. A few months before, I had accidentally cut my finger with a razor; the cut was really deep, so it bled and bled, and I remembered Grandpa's stomach and wondered how much you can bleed before you die. Never play with razors, Grandma liked to say, so I didn't tell her about that time. But this time I let her know. I had to admit I was also excited because I had become a woman. Grandma found me a half-empty dust-covered box of sanitary napkins that belonged to Mom. It upset me to use them, as if I'd acquired some aspect of womanhood that Mom had forfeited, as if I'd replaced her in some terrible way.

Mom's fancy dresses hung in the closet in my room. I liked to look at them and touch them, especially the rainbow-colored cotton dress and the shiny taffeta one with two skirts. The top skirt was black with hundreds of perfectly spaced little round holes in it. The underskirt was pink, so pink dots showed through. That was really clever, I always thought. The dresses reminded me of my mom in high heels, all dressed up, smelling of perfume and makeup, about to go out with Sam, looking her prettiest despite her disfiguring illness. Then one day my aunts came and divided up all of Mom's pretty things. I'd thought those dresses would hang in my closet forever, but now I sat on my bed, silently watching as they made their choices. Finally, one of my aunts looked at me. "You don't mind, do you?" I couldn't think of anything to say. I shook my head. None of the dresses fit me, so I assumed I had no claim to them—I couldn't keep them just because I liked to touch and feel them or because someday I'd grow big enough. I doubted that I would wear them anyway—it would be wrong to take Mom's place, to be glamorous like her, and so being glamorous became something to assiduously avoid.

One day, when I felt particularly lonely, I climbed into the double bed where Mom used to sleep and imagined her returning. I'd throw my arms around her and cry in bittersweet happiness. I absentmindedly reached down and touched myself. It felt nice, so I continued, and then an amazing sensation I'd never had before shook my entire body. In an instant my mind turned from thinking about Mom to thinking about having sex with a man someday. I was amazed by my discovery. Now I had my own way of making myself feel better whenever I wanted to, which turned out to be quite often. If at night I felt sad, or if I was upset about something, or if I couldn't fall asleep, or even if there was no real reason at all, I indulged in this private pleasure and didn't feel as bad about having to live without my mom. Maybe someday I'd have a man and children of my own, and then I could be part of a normal family again. To this day, I believe that my ever present sexual drive was a powerful life force that helped save me, and I'm grateful for it. Passion for what I had lost and for what was yet to come kept me going even in my bleakest moments. It fueled my desire to convert the tragedy of Mom's death into purpose and commitment through work, and allowed me to recognize how much I still longed to be close to other people.

Grandma was not much of an authority—Mom had always been in charge. Now I had to be in charge of myself, and sometimes I was scared that I'd do something bad and Grandma wouldn't be able to stop me. After all, she couldn't read, and when I brought documents home from school for her to sign, all she knew of their contents was what I told her. It took her nearly five minutes of painfully deliberate movement, pressing hard with a pen against the paper, just to sign her name. If I had wanted to, I could have made up a note saying I was sick and couldn't go to school, and get her to sign it. And then if we got letters from the school about my absence, I could lie about those, too. Really, if I wanted to I could be very, very bad.

But I never skipped school. In fact, I showed up early every morning, with special projects to show my sixth-grade teacher. With my friend Sarah, I made a cardboard model of a hospital, complete with an elevator operated by a string; with Rita I built a plaster of Paris model of the heart, and we spent hours discovering such fascinating facts as the amount of blood a heart will pump in a lifetime. We made charts and diagrams, and I worried that my own heart would stop beating, exhausted by all that pumping. Mrs. Kasnitz even showed our work to the principal, who wrote us a special note. I tried not to show how proud I felt. But the best thing about my projects was that they created the opportunity for these early-morning private conversations with Mrs. Kasnitz, and I couldn't imagine what my life would be like without them.

Sometimes Rita and I took the three-block walk to the public library, where we read books for hours, the perfect escape from our decaying surroundings. I'd finished off the science encyclopedias, cover to cover, but even though I was big now, I sometimes meandered into the children's book section and picked out the familiar ones I used to read with Mom. I especially liked *Millions of Cats*, with the black-and-white drawings of cats and kittens everywhere. The nice old lady and the nice old man who set out to find a kitten can take only one. So they ask the cats who's prettiest, and all the cats start to fight over that, all except one kitten who is too shy and scrawny to enter the fray. But that kitten is the only one to survive, and the old couple take her in and feed her until she's all plump and shiny and comfortable. "And it is a very pretty cat, after all," says the old woman. That kitten was smart enough to know that if you want to survive, it's a good idea to lay low.

Once in a while, we got to visit our brother Henry. "Mom had cancer," he blurted out one day as we sat in the sun on a huge rock right by the entrance to—as the bronze plaque on the rock informed us—the Pleasantville Cottage School. It had been a whole year now since Mom died, and maybe it was because her unveiling was approaching that Henry decided to let me know how it happened. His explanation was the first I had ever heard, but it didn't seem right to me. He insisted that he had learned the truth, but how could something that terrible be what Mom had? I had memorized the "Seven Warning Signs of Cancer" contained in those little brochures that seemed to turn up at school, in the doctor's office, everywhere. "A sore that does not heal" was the one I worried about the most. When I was littler, I was always falling down—climbing rocks and fences, balancing on the top rung of the jungle gym, taking pleasure in the anxieties of adult passersby ("Come down from there or you'll hurt yourself!" I didn't budge). When the scrapes on my knees didn't heal, I anxiously watched over them. Was it cancer? And if cancer had worried me all along, could it be that I once heard this explanation of Mom's illness? I tried to remember, but nothing came to me.

We hadn't seen Henry at the time of Mom's death. He went to Mom's funeral—he was thirteen, the Jewish age of manhood. Our family must have decided that Alexis and I were just babies, so they left us home. I could tell that my aunts and uncles were about to leave me out again, but this time I was smarter. "I want to go to the unveiling. I'm going to go. I'm old enough to go. You can't leave me behind. I have to go." You're too young, they tell me, and you can't understand. Understand what? I am thinking. Do they imagine that my mother has disappeared for a year and that I make nothing of it? That I haven't figured out what has happened? My relentless nagging finally made them give in, however reluctantly. And it went without saying that wherever I went, Alexis went, too.

The day of the unveiling came. I told them I wanted to stop

at a flower shop, to use the fifty cents I had saved to buy flowers. "Jewish people don't put flowers on the grave." Do I care
what Jewish people do? When you go to a cemetery, you put
flowers on the grave—I've read about it, I've seen it on TV
and in the movies. I've got to have my flowers. They finally
relented.

We arrived. I put my pretty yellow daffodils on the grave.
Everyone else picked ugly gray pebbles and put them on the
top of the headstone, the Jewish way. Ugly rocks. I was determined not to cry, to show them I was grown-up. When the
tears started to come, I took my sister by the hand and we
walked away from the grave site. We cried together where we
could not be seen. "We can't cry in front of anyone else," I
instructed my sister. Alexis had faith in the rules I'd made up
for us. Afterward, I overheard the adults explaining to one
another that Francine and Alexis hadn't cried because they
just didn't understand. The adults around us, intellectually or
emotionally incapable of imagining the intensity of our pain,
chose to imagine that we suffered none. Still, I was pleased. I
was where a dutiful daughter belonged, at the unveiling of my
mother's headstone marking the first anniversary of her death,
and I felt that I had, at least in some way or to some degree,
made up for missing her funeral.

After Sarah and Rita moved away, it required a lot more
effort to amuse myself. But we continued to see Sam. He came
most Sundays like he did when Mom was alive. He took
Alexis and me to the movies, then for ice cream or pizza. Yet
with Mom gone, our relationship was different. It was harder
to pretend that Sam was my dad. When we went to movie
theaters, I would read the marquee to Sam so he would know
what was playing. He liked the sexy movies, but I didn't, and
I tried to steer him away from them. I would lie about what

the marquee said, but it didn't do much good—he could tell what the movies were about from the pictures on display. One day we were walking home from a sexy movie. "Do you have any hair down there?" Sam asked. The question, which came out of nowhere, was tinged with a sexual tension. I pretended I hadn't heard him as I skipped ahead to catch up with my sister, but he had terrified me. And although Sam's intentions never became clear to me, I knew that I was no longer his little girl. From then on, I would keep my distance.

Still, I loved Sam. I felt very sad about always being on guard. I guess Mom was right. I shouldn't have carried on like I did. It wasn't safe, and now Mom wasn't here to protect me. And the guilt I felt that Mom had died and Sam now found me the attractive one would never leave me. Instead, it would become the basis for my self-imposed restrictions: resist competition with women, don't notice if they compete with you, never pursue another woman's man. Rules to live by.

My lucky number was five. I liked to count to five when I was nervous. Sometimes I'd do it silently dozens of times in a row. I was on my way to the dentist, who didn't use anesthesia. I walked, counting, one, two, three, four, five. Over and over again. This was supposed to make it hurt less. One day I was standing with Grandma in the drugstore. She was struggling to complete a transaction without speaking English. I started my silent mantra. One, two, three, four, five. Now I didn't even know why I was doing it. I guess just for good luck. Eventually, almost every quiet moment became an opportunity to repeat this reassuring ritual.

———

I'm applying for my residency training to become a psychiatrist, and my interviewer is a famous elderly psychoanalyst. It is 1973, a time when a student interview is license to conduct a psychiatric assessment. The analyst pulls out his pad and pencil and begins with my earliest memories. I tell him my story. "So did you develop any obsessions or rituals?"

"Not particularly," I reply. I have the impression he is unhappy with my answer. "Well, I used to count to five a lot, for good luck, and I'd step over cracks in the sidewalk."

"That's it?"

I can see where he's heading: he is measuring me against some theory which demands that my story include some good solid obsessive-compulsive behavior, and I worry that he is disappointed in me. "I had lots of troubles, though." I start to list them, doing my best to appease him with these substitute offerings. But the fact is there are no simple explanations for why some people react in one way to the events of childhood and others in another. There are too many factors—genes, environment, temperament, the fit between a parent and a child, the child's age when important events occur, and countless others of greater or lesser complexity. Despite the outward similarities of our upbringing, my brother and sister, when they speak of childhood, describe radically different worlds from mine. Henry had an angry mother, and Alexis had one she could barely remember. I felt the closest to Mom, the most like her, emulating her way of maintaining control, remaining connected to her even in death. Although each struggled to reestablish ourselves, their solutions to rebuilding a life would be different from mine. I would stay put, methodically reconstructing my life on top of the ruins, while Alexis and Henry roamed the world searching for answers elsewhere.

Grandma had now lost one child, but she continued to see her other three regularly, and they all lived nearby. Mostly we visited my Uncle Milton, who was my legal guardian, and his wife Milly. I also liked to see Aunt Anne and Uncle Jack, and I loved my six first cousins, all but one of whom were older than me. These visits with my family were usually fun, but sometimes they could be terrible. Grandma, Alexis, and I were sitting in the back of Milton's car when Alexis lamented that she hadn't cried when she learned of Mom's death. I was feeling guilty that I had told her the wrong way. Suddenly Milly turned around, yelling, "You have no reason to feel sorry for yourselves! Plenty of kids have it worse than you!" It was clear that Milly had missed the gist of the conversation, but I suspected that this was beside the point. I thought of Larry and his stubby arms, and how in our family there was no room to show distress over something so minor as Mom's death.

It didn't occur to me that money had to come from somewhere until my Uncle Milton, who arrived at the end of every month to write the checks for the rent and do whatever else needed to be done, began to shout at us. "Don't you know that your grandmother is using up all her Social Security money and even that's not enough?" I'd learned what Social Security money was, but I didn't know why this made him so mad at us. Maybe he was afraid he'd have to spend his own money. Maybe it was disconcerting to come every month and rediscover that no one was in charge here. Maybe it was because my grandmother and I fought every week over whether I could watch "Zorro" on TV. But I've done all my homework, I always explained. The fact that I got A's seemed to be of no relevance to our argument. Believe me, I was thinking as I

stared at Uncle Milton, I wish I could get a job, but I'm too
little. I'm supposed to finish school. But I said nothing. I was
very good at waiting out other people's rages.

Two years had passed since Mom's death, and gradually, without even realizing it, I fell into the same trap with Grandma
as I had with Mom. I assumed that life would go on like this
forever. But my aunts and uncles began to hint that this might
not be so. They mulled over the alternatives aloud, once dis-
tractedly suggesting that I live with "a rich old childless couple on Riverside Drive" whose identity they did not reveal.
Other times, they talked about themselves. "Would you like to
live with me?" Aunt Lillian asked during a three-day visit I
was having with Grandma and Alexis. Was that an invitation? Did I want to live with Lillian? I thought about Uncle
Hy and his penchant for inventing humiliating punishments
for the smallest of transgressions. One day he made me write
"I will respect my grandmother" one hundred times because I
had put on red socks when Grandma said to wear the white
ones. I considered refusing, but he was so much bigger and
meaner than me that I complied, suffering a humiliation I
would vividly remember for years. Even the adults in the family seem frightened of Hy. I was still staring silently at Lillian.
No, I was thinking, but I remained silent. I don't want to live
with any of you. I'm staying loyal to my mother. I'll live with
my helpless grandmother, thank you.
     Lillian elaborated. "It was your mother's dying wish that
you and your sister stay together, and I can take you because
you're older. But I can't take Alexis because I have to work."
Lillian had already raised her three children—two of them
were married with children of their own. She lived in a big

house. I was trying to follow her line of reasoning. She was making me an offer but informing me that it violated my mother's dying wish. I had the distinct impression that I was supposed to turn the offer down, but if that was the response she was looking for, I wasn't sure why she'd made the offer in the first place. I was scared. My thoughts became a jumble now. She wants me and doesn't want me, and I don't want to live with her, and I'm never agreeing to any changes ever again because I'm not giving up anything, and what are you trying to say to me anyway? But I did not speak aloud. I was good at saying nothing about something—my mother and I had perfected this technique. Saying something might just make it worse.

That night I crawled into bed to watch TV with my cousin Roberta, Lillian's middle child. I had been playing with her bubbly two-year-old son all afternoon. Roberta was beautiful, and I admired her long dark brown hair, her gentle manner, her soft voice. "I would take you to live with me if I could," she suddenly declared, and the idea had much greater appeal than her mother's confusing offer. Roberta was not that much older than I was—I could see she was an adult, but she was in some sense an adult who had not yet grown up. She had married very young, her husband was away in the Navy, and she was barely managing as it was. I knew it wasn't possible, but for a brief moment the fantasy enveloped me and I felt her warmth and tenderness. But then I let it go. It was too painful to contemplate the impossible, and I didn't want to make Roberta feel bad by looking to her for what she could not give me.

For many years I regretted my silence, convinced that if I'd only said the magic words—"Please keep me"—someone would have allowed me to stay. But then, more than thirty years later, during one of my futile attempts to make sense of the confusing events of my childhood by talking to my aunts and uncles, I realized that my memory was imperfect. Milly reminded me that she had made a proposal, one which I actually accepted.

It was 9:45 AM and we were poised at the door. "Remember," my Aunt Milly whispered in my ear, "the shoes are on the right, and we do them first." I was ready, I let her know, and my admiration for her scientific approach to shopping for bargains at Alexander's must have seemed obvious.

Aunt Milly talked so loud she always seems to be shouting. She had lots of dark brown hair; Milton was almost bald. Milly loved to boss Milton around. If Uncle Milton stood here, she told him to move over there; if he picked one chair, she ordered him to move to another. Poor Uncle Milton never seemed able to pick the right seat, not even in his own living room. When Milton was little, Grandma put him into little white dresses to photograph him—I'd seen the pictures, and I wondered if that was why he was such a sissy.

Milly and Milton had two sons, the younger exactly my age, but they were uninspired by their mother's craftiness. I knew she had pored over the newspapers and planned our strategies. The shoes were the best buy, at two dollars a pair. But only the most serious shopper would have even a chance of finding just the right size and style when the doors opened at ten and all the other scientific housewives descended on the shoe counter, where the pairs were jumbled in a pile in no order, with only a string connecting right and left shoes.

My Aunt Milly was a bona fide housewife, unlike my moth-

er, who had to work every day and sent us to the Jewish Ladies
Day Nursery when the school day ended. Milly could bake
cakes and cookies, and find the best bargains at Alexander's,
and sew on a bias. "What's a bias?" I asked her, and she taught
me the subtleties of hemming a skirt. "If the material flares out
at the bottom, when you hem it up, you have to make little
tucks every once in a while so it matches the upper material,
which is not as wide. Just like this." And she showed me how
it was done. A feeling of guilty pleasure ran through me: guilty
because I admired my aunt for the skills my mother never had,
and pleasure because the secrets of womanhood would now be
mine.

Milly seemed indomitable. We planned a picnic, but it
started to rain just as we were leaving. She looked at our disappointed faces and, without missing a beat, announced the
new concept of the Indoor Picnic, which she explained is
much, much better than the usual outdoor version. With great
fanfare, and giving the clear impression that this was what she
had really wanted to do all along, she spread the blanket on
the living room floor, unpacked the basket of food, handed
each of us a sandwich, and then sat back, hands clasped
behind her head, immensely pleased by this new development. It was infectious: her good nature in the face of what
seemed a disaster made the rainy afternoon seem even more
fun than if the sun had shone.

Milly and I became closer, and I lived in a rented cottage in
the country with her the summer of my thirteenth birthday.
For a short time, while Milton was at work in the city and my
sister was at camp, I even slept in the same double bed with
her. "Did you know you climb the wall with your feet at
night?" she announced. "No, I didn't know that!" I replied,
delighted that she had enough interest to notice something

about me that I had not even known myself. Milly taught me to knit, and I made an adorable sweater for my walking doll. The sleeves were blue with red trim, and the rest of the sweater looked like a rainbow because I knitted it with my favorite ball of yarn, the one that changed color every eight inches. Then Milly made the buttonholes and I sewed on gold buttons. I still own the sweater today. It's one of the few things from my childhood that I've carried with me all of my adult life, long after losing track of almost everything else.

Summer wore on. I felt a sexual tension I didn't understand, but soon I decided I must be in love with Milly's older son, my cousin Michael. Michael was very handsome, and he was always busy playing with his ham radio, trying to talk to complete strangers. He paid no attention to me whatsoever. He was fifteen, so a girl of thirteen was just a baby. Besides, he was my cousin. I developed the odd theory that maybe he would fall in love with me if he were missing a leg. Most of my central theories of life seemed to involve body parts, especially missing or defective ones. My ideas seemed crazy enough to me that I kept them to myself. Only much later would I understand how damaged and defective my parents' deaths had made me feel, and how convinced I was that only another damaged person could love me.

Aunt Milly and I baked almost every day. I didn't know whether it was the warm feelings generated by our making cookies together, or my wild crush on my cousin, but once in a while, not very often, I allowed myself to imagine joining Milly's family. Didn't Milly need a daughter? Wouldn't she make a nice new mother? On this last point, I held back a bit. Unlike my mother, Milly was intrusive, hovering, checking up on me. She would count the cookies in the jar to see if I had taken any before dinner; count my underpants in the laundry basket to make sure I changed them often enough to meet her high standards of personal hygiene. And yet Milly and I had fun together, something that rarely happened with my mother after she became ill. No, there was something else that worried me: the possibility that I could like her more than my own mother. Letting another take Mom's place might interfere with my self-assigned task: to keep my mother alive through a permanent mental effort to remember and long for her.

One day toward the end of the summer, alone in a room with me, Aunt Milly asked, "Would you like to live with me?" There was no mention of my sister, and I knew that she meant me, alone. I thought of my mother's dying wish that Alexis and I remain together, of what kind of daughter I would be if I abandoned my sister, of how wrong it would be to say yes. And then I said yes anyway.

A few weeks later, we drove to an unfamiliar destination in Manhattan. Aunt Milly, Uncle Milton, Alexis, and I entered an office to meet with a woman I had never seen before. I had no idea why we had come to this place, but the adults seemed to know what was going to happen, and I had the feeling that now I was about to be let in on the secret. The woman spoke. Alexis and I would be moving to a foster home, she informed us, to live with a family that had not yet been selected. As the words sank in, rage took over. "I'll jump off the Empire State Building," I shouted, striving for the most dramatic possible statement, one that would really have an effect. If I threatened something outrageous enough, they surely wouldn't go through with this. But they just humored me. The unfamiliar woman

described the virtues of a new home, but I had stopped listening. I could barely distinguish between the fury I felt toward my
relatives and the rage I turned on myself for being so helpless.
"You can't do this to me, you can't give me away if I don't want
to leave." I wished I really could jump off the Empire State
Building, but if I was to be loyal to my mother, I would stay in
control no matter what anyone did to me or how tempted I was
by my own anger. I took my mother's stoicism and self-control
as the model, and did my best never to deviate.

I have never learned by what process Milly's offer to live with
her was rescinded after I accepted it, or how my family concluded they would send me away. The foster care agency has
refused to show me records of the discussions that took place,
telling me only that it was my grandmother who insisted that
Alexis and I remain together. My Uncle Milton refused to
show me the letter my mother had written to him when she
designated him our legal guardian. Not that either of these
sources would necessarily have provided a satisfactory answer,
or erased my own explanation for the events: in saying yes, in
saying I wanted Milly to be my new mother, I committed a
crime of great magnitude. I was disloyal to my mother and sister. I understood the punishment: abandonment. I wiped
Aunt Milly's illicit offer from my mind completely, dredging it
up from memory only when Milly reminded me of it thirty
years later.

It is the summer before my fourth year in medical school, and
I've been hired for a project to discover why mothers sometimes fail to bring their children back for pediatric follow-up

appointments. The answer turns out to be quite simple: their children got better, so they didn't see any reason to return. But the obvious isn't what interests me. I read through many treatment records and make many home visits to this largely indigent minority population in New York City, and I am struck by how even the poorest and most disadvantaged families do their best to find places within the family for those children whose parents can no longer care for them.

How was my family different? I don't think any amount of reflection will ever allow me to understand why my relatives were so lacking in any sense of empathy or responsibility. My mother's three siblings, each married with children of their own, were not ill, unemployed, poverty-stricken, or drug-addicted. They were not estranged from my mother in any visible way. On the contrary, her social life consisted primarily of seeing them regularly. Was it possible she somehow understood that they would not come through for her in death any more than they had in life? When twice she found herself too overwhelmed to care for Henry, she had to turn to a foster care agency to help her instead of to her own siblings. The precedent had been set, and Alexis and I were condemned to follow it.

There was never anything troubling about any of this to my aunts and uncles. On the rare occasions I spoke to them as an adult, they expressed total perplexity that I would entertain the notion that their behavior had been anything other than exemplary. Uncle Milton informed me that while placing us in foster care was surely the best thing he could have done for us, he did make one mistake: he didn't do it soon enough. He let us live with our grandmother too long after she had become mentally incompetent. "We had only one bed," Uncle Milton explained every time I inquired. "You and your sister needed two beds, and that's what your foster mother had." For Uncle Milton, it was a question of furniture. He, just like our other aunts and uncles, would go to his grave without ever acknowledging—I think not even to himself—that he had abandoned us.

There must have been something wrong with me, I concluded, or my family wouldn't have given me away. In a sense, it was better if it was my fault, since I firmly believed that what I had caused I could surely correct. The adults in my family each deserted me in turn, and whatever the explanation—that I was unlovable, that I was being punished, that I was intolerably bad—whatever it was, I was to blame. Someday—and I was driven by this determination—someday, I would fix it.

Chapter 5

FAR FROM HOME

(1958–1959)

Alexis and I were assigned to the Rolls-Royce of foster care agencies: the Jewish Child Care Association would find a new home for my sister and me. We did not yet understand how lucky we were. Unlike many other foster care agencies, the JCCA, when the time came, would provide such middle-class luxuries as braces for our teeth, therapy for our spirits, and higher education for our minds.

Aunt Anne took me to an office somewhere near the East Side restaurant where she worked as a waitress, and I stood in a large open room with lots of chairs and desks. I was instructed to take a seat in a far corner, across a desk from a pretty, warm young social worker, smiling. She began to talk to me about going into foster care. I liked her, I was lonely, and I longed for someone to show an interest in what was happening to me. But I couldn't allow it. To do so would be to agree to my family's plans for me. We met three more times, and I started to feel fond of her, but I refused to show it. I sat in silent protest, resisting all overtures, no matter how tempting, thirsty at sea and only salt water everywhere.

We first met our foster parents in yet another office, the JCCA headquarters at Forty-fifth Street and Madison Avenue. Erma smelled nice—lots of perfume—and wore bright clothes and makeup. She greeted us cheerfully, then handed us each a present. Jack said hello quietly, then retreated into silence. It was tense as we opened our presents. Mine was a huge, half-length lacy slip, pretty and several sizes too big for me. Erma didn't like wasting money—she only bought oversized clothes, so her foster children could grow into them. At thirteen, however, I had already grown to one inch short of my full height. She smiled at us and expressed enthusiasm that we would soon be joining her family. There were already two other foster children: David, who was five, and Esther, a three-year-old. I wanted to be enthusiastic, too, but it wasn't working. I didn't want to leave my aunts and uncles and grandmother, I didn't want to live with Erma and Jack, and I didn't like Erma's useless present. I sat there—sorry for them that they would be stuck with me, and sorry for myself that I would be stuck with them. I mustered a smile and a few polite words, then felt relieved when our brief meeting ended. I went home to Grandma for a brief stay of execution, but the sentence was soon carried out.

The morning of my placement in foster care, I first went to

Madison Avenue to have a physical examination and, I imagined, do whatever else must be done to transform me into a foster child. I had trouble believing it was happening. I was a horse and they were checking my hooves and teeth. I saw myself being sold into slavery. Before I could go to the foster home, they had to examine me for defects and diseases. I wondered what they would do if they found any.

I was depleted now, exhausted, unable to make sense of this final separation from my family, beyond understanding how all the adults I was counting on could band together to exclude me. It was too painful to think about how their lives would go on without Alexis and me, go on as if we never existed. My outrage was muted by my growing detachment, my feeling that I was not fully alive. I took refuge in my firm control over my own behavior, my ability to carry out life's daily routines, however empty and meaningless they seemed. Without conscious effort or acknowledgment, I gradually obliterated any love I still had for the remaining members of my family. Eventually, even when I visited them, I felt as if I barely knew them, distant relatives I may have met once long ago, as irrelevant to my emotional life as I was to theirs.

The ride to my foster home was a funeral procession. Alexis and I sat in the backseat of an unfamiliar car with an unfamiliar driver; time passed in slow motion. I had no idea in what direction we were headed, nor how far or how long we drove. We arrived not at a cemetery but on the planet Mars. The tenement buildings I'd lived among all my life had been replaced with little private houses set close together. My foster family's was gray stone, the sunlight blocked by huge trees that overshadowed a brown lawn on which only a few clumps of green grass seemed capable of survival. There was hardly anyone on these streets—one little boy on a tricycle, one man tinkering with a car. Everyone here was white, and they all spoke English. There were no stoops to hang out on, no outdoor markets, no gangs, no knife fights on the sidewalks.

I knew I was supposed to like it, but I didn't. At thirteen, I didn't fit, not into any part of it. The customs did not suit me. I was utterly unathletic—I couldn't even ride a bike, and they didn't seem to know about roller-skating, the National Pastime of the South Bronx. When it was time to choose up sides, I was left for last with one or two other stragglers, the captains scratching their heads trying to figure out which one of us was likely to do the least harm. I couldn't stand touch football, and wherever the ball went, I made sure I was as far away as possible so that no one would blame me for what went wrong. Bowling might have been fun, if only I could have learned how to keep the ball out of the gutters. The only athletic pursuits I was good at were those in which I could substitute fear or tenacity for skill. I was a good runner, and when we climbed ropes in gym, I set the record for time spent suspended in air. Run for your life and never let go: words to live by.

My clothes were all wrong, too, although I tried to replace my flowery cotton skirts with the subdued wools these people seemed to favor in November. In the South Bronx, there were no "summer" and "winter" clothes. We just had "clothes," and when it got cold, you put on more of them.

"Don't worry about this test," the English teacher told me as she handed out the questions on my second day at school. I was pleased by her look of surprise when she returned the paper with a grade of 95. That was what I was good at—most of the time it seemed the only thing I was good at. A bad grade would have been cause for total panic. Fortunately, I rarely had to confront that problem. I knew how to study, how to prove I was as capable as children who still had parents, how to triumph over the boys by beating them out with my near perfect grades in math and science, how to elicit from teachers the adult praise and admiration I was so desperate for. But even more important, I knew how to enter other worlds through books and make my present world go away, pretending for a while that I was not really in this time and place, separated from everything safe, from everything familiar, from everything I once loved.

"You can call me Mom now," Erma said, commanding, almost threatening, after I got into bed one night. She had dropped her cheerful demeanor, staring at me with contained rage for not having come to this conclusion on my own. I suddenly had a sinking feeling, trapped here with a terrifying witch, nowhere to turn. I averted my gaze and then, desperate, converted my sense of helplessness into rage, answering Erma only with an internal monologue: To me, you're nobody. I've been here only two weeks and I haven't felt comfortable for a minute. I still have a mother, anyway, even if she's dead. My mother needs to live through me now, and I'm prepared to devote myself to this task, to stay loyal and always remember lest she cease to exist. I don't need another mother, and it wasn't my idea to come here in the first place. I looked up. Erma was still standing over me, waiting, and I was still scared. I did as Erma said, spitting the word out, feeling thoroughly insincere, then silently apologizing to Mom for using her name. My heart began to harden against Erma.

Like other children following the death of a parent, I had reconstructed my world using the remaining relationships I

still had with my family. But now, except for my sister, everyone and everything familiar was gone: my aunts and uncles,
my grandmother, Sam, the library and the park, my apartment
and nearly all my possessions, my school, my classmates. Faced
with such a sudden and complete loss, I clung even more res-
olutely to my dead mother, but I was even worse off than on
the day she died: I had reluctantly made an effort to replace
her with Milly, but it had failed miserably, and I had no plan
to try again. Esther and David had arrived at Erma's house as
toddlers, happy to have found a new mother, but I was an adolescent, too old to embrace a stranger in that way. The more
aggressively Erma came after me, the more I retreated into my
protective shell.

The tension between us was unrelenting, so I held on to a
faint hope that my aunts and uncles would change their minds
and come back for me. But they did not. I began to feel pro-
gressively more unhappy, enraged and emotionally numb,
unable to grasp how I could be both at once. My mind lost its
normal sense of order; fragments of misery floated through it,
ungrounded in time or place. This disorganized state bore no
relation to my previous grief. I was more lost than ever. I con-
structed a wall around myself, which I hoped was impenetra-
ble. Inside this wall, there was one other living human: my little sister, the person for whose sake, presumably, I had been
banished to this place. But where once I had taken pride in all
the ways I helped my mother by taking care of my sister, keeping her at my side wherever I went, now I hated her. She was
all that was left of my past, and there was no one else close
enough to hate. Mostly I contained these feelings, but once I
lost control and, in a frenzy of yelling and screaming at her,

threw all of her books out of the bookcase and onto the floor. After I calmed down, I was ashamed and remorseful. For my sister, I was the parental extension of Mom and Grandma, the only piece of a caretaker that remained from her past. I felt this obligation as I struggled to control my rage—no one was watching to keep me from harming her.

I made a conscious effort to divide my misery into two parts—home and school. When I was at home, I resisted thinking about how I didn't fit in with the other kids at school. And when I was at school, feeling awkward and left out, I refused to think about how miserable I was at home. This way, I had to contend with only half my troubles at one time. I became good at putting things into compartments.

Often I skipped breakfast, and in the winter I usually forgot to put on some essential article of clothing, like gloves or socks, so I set off on the eight-block walk to school cold and hungry. It was amazing I existed at all, I mused as I walked along. With all the millions of sperm my father had produced, and all the hundreds of eggs my mother had made, the odds against my being here seemed overwhelming. Halfway to school, I passed the Long Island Rail Road station and stopped inside the waiting room to buy a chocolate bar and let my hands and feet warm up. I promised myself that I'd remember to dress warmly the next time, but I almost never did. I could feel the raging war between my feelings of self-hatred and my powerful instinct for self-preservation. And I didn't really know if the cold stinging sensation in my hands and legs was a form of self-punishment or a remedy for my numbness.

I still saw my family from time to time. Alexis and I made the trek alone to Aunt Lillian's house every third Sunday, two long bus rides to visit Grandma, who, when we were placed in foster care, was taken in by her oldest living daughter.

Grandma must have once been very powerful, because they didn't dare send her away. Despite their bickering over whose turn it was to bear the burden, my aunts and uncles would keep Grandma until she died at ninety-one, incapable of recognizing the members of her own family. Such was Grandma's control over her children, and, perhaps, over Alexis and me as well, since we felt obliged to abide by the visiting schedule worked out by the JCCA at Grandma's behest. We would arrive in Elmont, Long Island, at 2 P.M., and Lillian and Hy would make themselves scarce. Then Grandma would cry to us, the same old refrain, "It's as if you were born from my own body! How can a daughter die before her mother?" After exactly two hours of this, at 4 P.M., we would leave, right on schedule, and give thanks during the silent car ride back with Uncle Hy that it would be three weeks before we had to carry out the perfunctory ritual yet again. Once in a while, I was invited to a gathering of my entire family, where I went through the motions, polite and utterly detached. What felt most real was my sense that I carried Mom (and sometimes my dad, too) with me everywhere I went, a little homunculus inside my brain. Mom participated in all my activities, living on through me.

Just as the psychoanalytic theories posit, my mourning, unlike that of an adult, consisted of holding on to my dead mother even more tightly than in life, rather than moving further away from her. When I realized there would be no acceptable substitute, I redoubled my efforts to stay conscious of Mom, to re-create her, to use her in place of any living relationship. It was much less frightening than facing just how alone I really was.

I was aware of my detachment, and ashamed of being so impaired. I remembered a more successful self, laughing, having fun, playing with my friends, enjoying other people. But this was no longer who I was. I'd become someone else, all normal sense of continuity having been disrupted. What was left was to maintain a facade of normality, in communion with my mother, who had mastered the art of putting on a show of strength when you fear that all you are is weakness. I would spend years of my adult life working to unlearn these techniques for maintaining distance and control so that I could reconnect to people. But for now, I was thinking only of survival.

Trauma. Posttraumatic stress disorder. When I am a psychiatrist, these are the labels I'll learn to describe my state of mind as a foster child. Trauma occurs when a serious threat presents itself, but action is of no avail—neither resistance nor escape is possible. The ordinary ways of coping become overwhelmed, disorganized, and fragmented. Systems of attachment and meaning are disrupted. Faith in life's order and continuity is lost and the world becomes unsafe. There is a waning sense of one's positive value as a human being. Development is arrested, or even reversed, and the traumatic response may persist indefinitely, causing profound personality changes. The affected person is obliged to reenact the traumatic event as if it were a contemporary experience, instead of remembering it as something in the past.

I found it easy to identify with the descriptions—the disorganization, the psychic numbing, the feeling of living in constant danger, the guilt about survival, the conviction that one is permanently damaged, the sense of worthlessness, the struggle to believe in a future. I have felt all this myself.

The degree of trauma caused by the loss of a parent in

childhood varies. For me, the deaths of both my parents, while extremely painful, were not as traumatic as the abandonment by my family that followed. It was something like the experience of a navy veteran patient of the well-known psychoanalyst Abram Kardiner, who studied the experiences of men traumatized by battle. The man's ship was sunk by enemy fire, and he spent twelve hours in the water before a torpedo-boat destroyer arrived for a rescue. Following normal military procedure, the boat picked up the officers first, even though they were relatively safe in the lifeboat. The enlisted men, including the patient, hung on to the raft and were passed over, some of them drowning as they awaited their turn. This perceived abandonment by his fellow soldiers—his own family— was more traumatic to him than any other aspect of his ordeal. Despite my many fantasies to the contrary, the rational part of me understood that my parents could not prevent themselves from dying. But my aunts and uncles' indifference made me feel as utterly worthless and expendable as this sailor must have felt clinging to the life raft.

There is some debate over whether trauma is caused by the unfortunate events themselves, or by each person's unique approach to making sense of them. It seems to me that there is little reason to set up such a dichotomy. Tragic external events and fantastic and highly personalized explanations for them coexist. The events of my own life were clearly very real, and from my perspective very horrible. But the explanations I came up with for them were even worse.

"Maybe she should leave. I don't want her here." Every night I sat listening at the top of the stairs near the room my sister and I had been assigned—our foster parents and the two smaller children all lived downstairs, where Alexis and I were not permitted after 8 P.M. Banished. A year had passed since I had come here, and Erma was in a constant rage at me. She'd never asked for a teenager, she told me, only a child Alexis's age. I came along in the bargain. Not only had I failed to love her as a daughter, but she felt I stood in the way of her relationship with my sister. How ironic that Erma wanted to compete with me for a role I had now come to hate: carrying out my mother's dying wish by taking care of Alexis. Every night I eavesdropped on her angry conversations with Jack, but it was always the same. Maybe I listened in to try to determine whether I was staying or leaving.

An employee of the foster care agency—someone I never saw before or after—showed up to talk to Erma and me. "Do you want to leave?" she asked me. I thought of my brother and the horrible stories he'd told me about having to eat with the dog in the basement. I thought of my inability to provide even the most basic necessities for myself. How could I be sure it would be any better somewhere else? At least this place provided structure and physical safety, and the familiar, however problematic, seemed better than the unknown. If I couldn't love or be loved, what difference did it make where I was living?

I knew I was ugly and hateful. No child with even the least bit of appeal could be rejected this many times. "You have less personality in your whole body than Esther has in the tip of one finger," Erma repeatedly told me, comparing me with my now four-year-old foster sister. Esther was unbelievably sweet and sympathetic, and I liked her very much. She had come here with her brother David when she was two and he was four. All I knew of her former life was that her parents were very fat, and that they had neglected their children. Since Esther was much too young for me to compete with, I took it that the invidious comparison was just Erma's way of saying she hated me. Believe me, I was thinking, you can't hate me half as much as I hate myself. You're not the first person to shout at me in utter frustration, and when my mother did it, her neck veins bulged. But I loved my mother, and I don't even like you. I was down to the basics of survival: food and shelter. Don't worry, I told myself, although I was always worried. Someday you'll grow up and be able to take care of yourself.

Finally, the foster care lady presented it to me: "Erma doesn't want you here, but she's not going to make you leave. Stay if you want." Not much of an invitation, and yet Erma had given me my first opportunity to participate in determining where I would live. I hated my situation, but I decided to stay. Maybe Erma somehow understood my decision as proof that I did want her after all, maybe she was acting on the same impulses that would later lead her to take in dozens of stray cats despite her professed distaste for them, maybe she felt some sense of obligation to an orphaned child which my own family could not feel—maybe it was these things that prevented her from taking the final step of asking to have me removed. Whatever the explanation, the crisis had passed, although it would be a long time before Erma's anger fully abated. And my inclusion in an honest discussion of my future was a turning point. At last I felt I was being treated as a capable person, able to hear an unpleasant truth. It was a hard lesson, but it helped me to accept my own responsibility for making the best of my circumstances.

I have a colleague who works as a judge in a Brooklyn family court. Here, hundreds of traumatized children are shuttled back and forth every day between parents who abuse or neglect them and temporary foster homes. She agrees with my impression that still today children are plopped down into foster homes, or even moved from one to another, as if things will all fall into place quite naturally. They are given little realistic help with adjusting—not that it is so clear what realistic help would consist of, or how children could be persuaded to accept it. As far as I was concerned, the foster care agency had uprooted me from my family, and they were on the side of the enemy. I did my best to resist offers of assistance, trusting no one in authority.

"What's that?" the psychologist asked me. We sat together in a small room at the JCCA Madison Avenue headquarters. Patient and soft-spoken, she was pointing to an inkblot with two dancing figures that clearly seemed to have both penises and breasts, but her finger was on the penis. "I don't know," I replied. She seemed incredulous, and challenged my answer. I knew how to refuse to budge. I was good at it. Refusal was one of the few powers I felt certain of. Don't waste your time, I was thinking. Of course, any teenage girl knows what a penis is, but I'm never going to tell you that word. The psychologist persisted in her quest, as if my response to this particular question was of critical importance. But I'd become just as stubborn as on the day I refused to eat Mom's poison-mushroom soup. I was on strike.

The real object of my strike was Miss Kaufman, the social worker who came to our foster home too much for my taste, and who lay in wait for me as I returned from school. Middle-aged and alone, traveling through life without a family, free to intrude into the lives of pathetic people like us, by her very existence she reminded me of a reality I'd just as soon have forgotten. I did my best to tell her nothing at all.

"Wally, did you ever tell your social workers anything?" Wally and I were on one of our five-hour round-trip excursions to Albany, where I was to meet with officials of the State Office of Mental Health.

Big Wally, as he is universally known, has worked for me on the community service program at the Psychiatric Institute for more than twenty years. He was the youngest of eight children. He never met his father, at least not that he remembers, and lived with his mother in the South until he was five. Then his mother was committed to a mental hospital, never to return, and he grew up in an unpleasant foster home from which he periodically escaped. Wally has seen a lot: violence, gangs, drugs, gambling, even the inside of a jail. But he has overcome his problems—not without difficulty and setbacks—and made a life for himself.

He is, according to personnel records, our driver, but this doesn't even begin to describe his place in our operations. He repairs plumbing equipment and electrical wiring, delivers food and medicine to our clinics, does carpentry work, runs interoffice mail from one site to another, oversees our cleaning services, drops off blood specimens for the lab, and, at six feet and 260 pounds, he makes a splendid escort through some of the meaner streets of our Washington Heights neighborhood. You name it, Wally is on call by beeper twenty-four hours a day to do it. He is not only hard-working but smart and observant as well. I once asked him how he made it. "Everyone told me I'd be nothing, nobody, a nut like my mother. I was never going to let that happen to me. I let myself fall just so far. Then I catch myself."

Wally and I have talked a lot during these long car rides. We started years ago with a subject we had to get out of the way before we could move on: the conflicts between blacks and Jews. His stories about bigotry, particularly against black men, were shocking, even when I sometimes sensed a slightly paranoid edge to them. Then one day Wally called me a "rich doctor" once too often and I told him my story about being orphaned and growing up in foster care. He was genuinely surprised, and for the first time told me that he was a foster child, too. That settled it: we had a common heritage; we were more alike than different.

"Tell the social worker anything? No, social workers don't know what's going on anyway. If the foster parents have a nice house and take care of their own kids, they think they take care of the foster kids, too. They see you wearing beat-up clothes while the other kids have nice clothes, but they never realize that you get second-rate treatment in everything else, too. You're going to tell the social worker about it? That'll make it worse. The social worker goes away, but you have to stay there and live with these people."

"Do you have friends?" Miss Kaufman inquired. "Yes, I have friends," I replied, knowing full well that I merely went through the motions of having friends, and had lost all ability to feel genuinely close to anyone new. "Why don't you hang up pictures of your mother?" she nagged yet again, the same boring topic. I was totally silent. You fool. Don't you know I don't even own a picture of my mother? Don't you know I was sent to this place without any of my mother's possessions, all of which were taken by my aunts and uncles? Don't you see that my foster mother is in a rage at me for not embracing her as my new mother? Do you want me to go out of my way to inflame her further? But I said nothing. She talked on and on. "Shut up. Shut up!" I finally screamed, setting the tone for all our subsequent after-school conversations. Finally, after all my carrying on, Miss Kaufman referred me for psychological evaluation.

"She's horrible," I explained to the psychiatrist across the desk from me. There's nothing wrong with me—just give me a new social worker and I'll be fine. And believe me, I was thinking, you can sit here all day and that's all you'll get out of me. I had no idea what they concluded about my mental health, but to my amazement and pleasure, they gave me a different social worker! For the second time, the JCCA allowed me some say in who my caretakers would be. I had won the contest of wills with Miss Kaufman, and I was very pleased.

"Did you know people masturbate in closets? Did you know sex is good and fun if you want to have it with someone?" My new social worker was full of stories. She would chain-smoke while telling them, ignoring the emphysema her doctors said was killing her. She was in love with two men and couldn't decide between them, so she gave them both up and found a new one. Her first husband died of TB, and while she nursed him during his final illness, she became addicted to his pain medication. But her father cured her by keeping her locked up in his house and drunk for the first two months after her husband died. And all this had happened in Austria! Her next husband died, too, but now she had still another one whom she called by his surname. I took this to be an exotic European habit.

Erma wasn't pleased by all this talk. She didn't care whether this woman had three husbands or ten. She wanted to know the facts. When was our clothing allowance coming? When were the doctors' appointments? But I was relieved. My new social worker didn't demand that I reveal anything, and I loved her exotic stories.

I had settled in, and for better or worse, I was here to stay in a world entirely different from the one I had known. Now I could begin to come to terms with the dramatic and eccentric new family I had so reluctantly joined.

Chapter 6

F O S T E R   F A M I L Y

(1 9 5 9 – 1 9 6 4)

Jack was a shoe salesman. He was tall and thin, with a grav-
elly voice that made him sound as if his nose was always
slightly stuffed up. He worked in Jamaica, Queens, a part of
New York City that people on Long Island considered frightening and dangerous, even though it was much tamer than
the South Bronx. He hardly ever spoke, and I wondered how
he managed to talk to his customers. His favorite activity was
watching baseball on television. In fact, he had played minor-
league baseball as a young man. He drove his car oddly: very
slowly, with one foot on the brake and one on the accelerator

at all times. Every evening he counted the silverware, just to make sure none of it had accidentally fallen into the garbage. Jack had three sisters. Two of them were married, and none had children. The unmarried one had some mysterious mental illness. Sometimes she would take off all her clothes and run naked in the street, after which she would wind up in a psychiatric hospital. Jack's other sisters seemed quiet and a little odd. I wondered if they had no children because odd people weren't very likely to.

Jack's wife Erma, by contrast, was lively and talked constantly, rattling off one dramatic story after another. She had brown hair, a plump body, and large breasts which she would periodically threaten to have surgically reduced. Erma's mother had died, and her father was old and selfish. She claimed her younger brother Lou always got more love and attention. When her father died, her brother also got most of the money, not that there was very much of it, but it bothered her in principle. She said her father didn't consider her foster children to be his real grandchildren—they didn't have the same status as Lou's two daughters, his real biological descendants.

This distressed Erma. She had no biological children. Maybe she couldn't have any, but she never told me that. Maybe she didn't want to have children with Jack because she feared that his sister's madness was hereditary. Maybe they didn't even have sex—that was another one of my theories. They slept in the same bed, but Erma said Jack flailed his arms about in his sleep (she illustrated with comic gesticulations), and she told us he snored, too. I felt sure she wouldn't want to have sex with someone who was doing all that.

Erma had some unusual beliefs. For instance, she said—and I could never tell how serious she was—that humans had come from another planet a long time ago. The proof of this, she claimed, is that they have a natural aversion to snakes and spiders, the only life forms we humans found when we landed in our spaceships. I'd learned from my days with Grandma to listen to adults' favorite theories with quiet acceptance, and I never engaged Erma in debate, at least not on these points.

Erma was very creative. She made her own clothes and multicolored rugs for the floors, she wove elaborate tapestries and hung them on the walls, she made dolls even more beautiful than the one I'd given my mom. Her dolls had dresses with long trains and intricate designs with hundreds of beads and sequins. Once she even won a $1,000 prize in a doll-making contest. We were all very proud of her for this, even though it happened before we met her. She used the money to buy a new stove and refrigerator, a real spending spree for her, since she normally was a great penny-pincher—she liked to buy cakes that were past their expiration date and one-half off, and the dented cans of vegetables that sold for ten cents.

Erma was constantly fixing up her house, and the place was always in the middle of some elaborate and unconventional construction project, never finished. One day she decided the living room should look like a Gothic castle, so she made tapestries with lords and ladies and knights on them and stuck them on the walls. She furnished the room with hard, uncomfortable wooden benches, because she thought they looked authentically medieval. She rolled her eyes at the suggestion of anything sexual between her and Jack, but then fixed up her bedroom by tacking red cloth to the walls and putting in lamps with red lightbulbs. "Looks like a nineteenth-century brothel, doesn't it?" she said, laughing with some pride. If you didn't like one of Erma's designs, no problem—she'd soon renovate it all over again anyway. Even with all her strange impulses and varied tastes, she did have artistic talent and imagination. But you had to be prepared for some truly astonishing home-decorating innovations.

One day, as a special treat, Erma took us out to eat at a Chinese restaurant. I'd never seen Chinese food before, and I had no idea what to order. She picked shrimp chow mein for me, and they brought it out in an exotic-looking metal dish on a pedestal. I opened the top and picked out some mushy-looking vegetables, assiduously avoiding the suspicious-looking shrimp. But Erma insisted I have some shrimp—it's the best part, she explained, heaping a bunch of them onto my plate. Since there was no way I was going to put those things in my mouth, I used my old Bronx technique: the minute Erma looked the other way, into my shoe they went. "Aren't they good?" Erma smiled when she glanced at my shrimp-free plate. I nodded guiltily, ashamed of my plan, soon accomplished, to dispose of this delicacy in a Chinese restaurant's toilet bowl. Fortunately, we usually ate at home.

On holidays, Erma would invite her family over for dinner—she had to, she explained, because no one else ever volunteered. There was always her father, and her brother with his wife and daughters. Sometimes Jack's sisters came, plus an assortment of other people whose exact relationship to Erma I was never able to discern. Then she would cook all day, making dozens of different dishes. No matter how fussy an eater you were, you were guaranteed to find something you liked among all these plates and bowls and platters. Erma's taste in table settings was yet another source of wonder. Sometimes the table was set up to look really fancy; other times it wasn't set at all. Once she invited some important guests who had never met her before. There were so many of us that she decided to serve the food on the Ping-Pong table in the basement. She summoned everyone downstairs, took down the little Ping-Pong net, and proceeded to spread a double-bed sheet over the table, since no conventional tablecloth could cover the expanse. We all sat down, trying to figure out how we were going to carry on a conversation with the person sitting on the opposite sideline. Reaching across the field of play to set the table was out of the question, so when it came time to distribute silverware, Erma simply arrived with an armful of cutlery, dropped it in the middle of the playing surface, and shouted, "Everyone grab a fork!" Our fancy guests looked on in horror; I was just barely successful in repressing the urge to burst out laughing.

Ordinary pets were not for Erma, either. At first she didn't have any animals at all, but one day, with no prior warning, she came home with two tiny brownish-yellow ducklings. They were adorable, and in what seemed like no time at all, they grew into enormous white ducks. Erma, who had been keeping them inside the house, finally had to concede that they belonged outside. So she set them up in the garage. By this time Elmer and Selma (these names rhyme where I come from, and I guess Erma thought they did, too) had imprinted on Erma. They followed her on walks around the block, quack-quack-quacking, which everyone found quite amusing, except the police, who stopped her on one of her perambulations to inform her that it is not legal to keep farm animals in Lynbrook, New York. The heat was on.

"They're going to arrest my ducks," Erma declared when the cops departed. But she had already devised a scheme to keep Elmer and Selma out of jail: we would drive them over to the duck pond and give them their freedom. We packed the ducks into the car and started out. All the way over, Erma was worrying about whether Elmer and Selma would be able to adapt to living in the wild with all those other ducks, whether there was some kind of duck orientation period they should go through before being released. Elmer and Selma just kept quacking. I never knew ducks could quack so loud.

We arrived and put them at the edge of the pond. In thirty seconds, the two of them had disappeared into the crowd of entirely identical white ducks. Did they adjust? Did they learn to get along with the other ducks? Did they miss Erma? Were they ever homesick? We never found out. But as we watched her distress at having to let them go, the connection between Erma's devotion to her foster ducks and her devotion to her foster children was not lost on us.

Erma didn't suffer in silence like Mom did. So when she couldn't figure out where David had gone, she would routinely call the police in a panic. "Oh, hello, Mrs. Jacobs," they would respond calmly, familiarly, and then agree to issue an all-points bulletin. Why couldn't David remember to tell her where he was going? Now the patrol cars were circling the neighborhood, loudspeakers blasting: "Be on the lookout for a seven-year-old boy, brown eyes, curly brown hair, wearing blue denim shorts and a white-and-yellow-striped shirt." David would hear the announcement that it was time to come home, and emerge from a door three houses down the block.

Ambulance sirens are blaring, and I am the third-year medical student on the trauma team. I race with the trauma surgeons to the emergency room. Twelve-year-old boy, jumped onto the back bumper of a city bus for a ride, then fell off. Blunt trauma, we call it, since there's no visible injury, but only the as-yet-unknown consequences of falling onto the street from a perch on the bumper of a moving bus. Onto a stretcher he goes, up to the second floor for an emergency X ray, onto the cold X ray table, equipment moved into place. He stares at us, not moving, not saying a word. Suddenly he goes into cardiac arrest. The call for more help goes out over the public-address system, and a herd of doctors and nurses descends, but too late. He has bled to death from a ruptured spleen. The spleen, essential in fighting infection, is filled with thousands of blood vessels. When it ruptures, death can follow within minutes. We go through a ritual of self-recrimination for missing what went wrong, followed by attempts to console one another: every doctor in the room has made mistakes, including fatal ones. I'm still shocked by the rapidity of the child's death, and by the magnitude of the punishment for this one reckless act. I think of the mother, waiting for her child to return home, not yet knowing that he lies dead on an X-ray table in a hospital. No wonder Erma worried so much.

Erma took in still one more child, four-year-old Alan. He was the first to arrive solo, rather than as one of a pair. This was his second foster home, and it would turn out that this one would be permanent. Erma would get many more offers to take in other people's troubled half-grown children, but for her five was enough.

Erma didn't like being called by so many different last names—her own and that of each of her foster children. She said people thought foster parents did it for the money, and she resented this. It wasn't enough money to do it for that reason, she explained. She had spent her own money fixing up the house for us. She asked for children who were going to stay permanently, not go back and forth between foster homes and their biological parents. We were her children. She felt that, and she meant it.

Despite Erma's devotion and her lively sense of humor, despite her reassuring commitment that I could stay, our relationship remained unhappy, and neither of us saw any way out. She was profoundly disappointed in me, and expressed her fury bitterly, with the same dramatic flair that in other circumstances made her so funny and lively. Why didn't I notice when the house was dusty and clean it up? Why didn't I have as much personality as Esther? Why did I ask for more money than the agency gave her? Why did I stay up late at night to do my homework, running up her electric bill? I couldn't provide any satisfactory answers. Her anger fortified my need to remain withdrawn, so I stayed numb. My lack of affection left her chronically dissatisfied and reinforced her anger. Erma's efforts to win Alexis over, which included a campaign to turn her against me, left Alexis feeling betrayed. My sister couldn't figure out how to get what she needed from either one of us, and would emerge from our foster home feeling angry and distant. Erma continued to hold me accountable. So it went, a closed circle none of us seemed able to penetrate.

I had my techniques for dealing with Erma, though. One was the drive-her-crazy-by-stonewalling-her technique. I would watch her scream and yell and lose her cool and I would say nothing. This was a natural outgrowth of my earlier methods of dealing with adults, but the goal then was to appease. Now it was to provoke.

Another method was the sneak-about strategy. For example, I would turn the lights off at 10 P.M. like Erma said, and sit in the hallway doing my homework under the forty-watt bulb left on as a night-light. Is it really true that reading in dim light ruins your eyes? Listen carefully for Erma's footsteps coming up the stairs. Jump back into bed with all your books and pretend to be asleep. As soon as she leaves, go right back to work.

Nevertheless, Erma was there when something scary happened. I was walking around barefoot despite her constant admonitions to wear slippers, and I stepped on a needle. I reached down to pull it out and, to my horror, came up with only half of it. The other half was still buried in my foot, inaccessible, and I was convinced I was a goner: I well remembered the story of a woman who had a needle in her foot that traveled to her heart and killed her! Erma rushed me to the hospital. The surgeon explained that I had to stay overnight for an operation—they were going to put me to sleep, cut into my foot, and take out the piece of metal embedded in it. Put me to sleep? Cut into my foot? They're going to slice off my leg, that's what they're going to do! What am I going to do with only one leg? But when I awoke, my leg was still attached, the needle was gone, my foot was bandaged, and I spent the next three weeks walking around on crutches. I needed Erma. She had come to the rescue in an emergency and then, graciously and selflessly, cared for me during my convalescence.

It wasn't until well into my adult life that I realized how rejected Erma felt, and how little she understood that, like any thirteen-year-old, I was trying to separate from my parents, not acquire a new set. I was faced with a task not in the ordinary developmental sequence of events—to connect at just the moment it feels more important to disconnect. We had no common history to fall back on—we hadn't known each other when I was little, and needy in a very different way. Orphaned adolescents have a terrible dilemma: they have a developmental need to break away, but their parents have beaten them to the punch. Continued adult involvement in my life was essential, and yet it was the wrong time to begin again. As much as I wanted and needed help, I fought just as hard for my independence.

Erma knew rejection, too. Her own parents had greatly favored her younger brother over her. They had never supported her attempts to pursue her considerable artistic talents. Maybe my inability to love her was a painful reminder of how she didn't measure up. From my perspective, her hatred of me was proof that I'd killed my parents and been banished by my family for all my wrongdoing. I deserved to be punished. She had her interpretation of the facts, I had mine. Later we would both regret that two people who needed and wanted to connect couldn't figure out a good way to do so. She would apologize, and I would express gratitude that someone in the world was willing to give me what my own family was not: a place to live until I could grow up.

I got a three-week reprieve from my foster-home troubles when I attended sleep-away camp for the last time, and I had a chance to briefly recapture who I once was. Camp Hurley in Kingston, New York, was supposedly staffed by Communists. Is that why we had a written schedule of activities but were never required to do any of them? Mostly we sat in the woods and smoked cigars because we couldn't seem to get cigarettes, or else we sat in our bunks and read dirty stories. At night we danced to the Platters or Johnny Mathis, although I couldn't figure out how girls were supposed to guess which way boys were going to move so that they could follow. I tongue-kissed a boy for the first time, but I found it disgusting. When we weren't doing these things, we went boating on the lake with our counselors, who kept telling us stuff about the workers of the world, but we never really understood what they were getting at. I mingled unself-consciously with kids who were black and Hispanic, and no one seemed to care what anyone's race was. This left a profound impression on me. But most important, I felt pleasure again, which I hadn't known since I'd arrived at my foster home.

Boarding school or camp, under the right circumstances, can be a refuge for parentless teenagers. Here, an adolescent whose parents are absent or dead is not really distinguishable from those around him who have parents waiting at home. In some sense, this is a place where no one has parents. When these institutions are well run, they offer a ready supply of well-intentioned adults to give praise, express concern, and provide opportunities to learn the skills that make young people into disciplined and independent adults. Art Buchwald, who spent his childhood in orphanages and foster homes, seems to have felt this way about joining the Marines at seventeen: "The Marine Corps was the best foster home I ever had."

Big Wally would understand. He was sixteen and living in Harlem, surrounded by violence and drugs, when he saw an ad on TV about a residential school for teenage boys looking to escape this environment. He signed up for two years. "We lived there, in the country, in upstate New York. It was the best thing that ever happened to me. They gave us everything—counseling, discipline, job skills, self-respect. They even taught us how to dress for an interview. It worked. We all did well. That's why they closed the program. They don't want to see black men succeed."

For Wally in his school, for Art Buchwald in the Marines, for me in my summer camp—at least for the time we were there, not having parents didn't seem so important.

After camp, I discovered boys in earnest, but my approach was haphazard. I accepted a first date with a boy I didn't like, and we went to the movies. Every time he put his arm around me, I felt insects crawling up my skin. "Don't do that," the little round woman usher admonished him. He removed his arm. Then he put it back. I waited for the usher to return and tell him to stop, and the cycle started all over again. When the movie ended, he walked me home, and dozens of phone conversations about another date followed. I didn't say yes, and I didn't say no. I had a crush on a boy who turned out to be gay, and then a short-lived romance with a car mechanic who liked to drink beer while he drove. During my date for the freshman prom, the only words exchanged all night occurred when I finally managed to choke out, "I like your tie." I dated two boys both named Steve, and at home we called them "Steve Number One" and "Steve Number Two." Once one of them came to pick me up and my foster sister Esther shouted up the stairs, "Steve Number Two is here!" Eventually, I settled on a nice tall Irish boyfriend who really liked me and even talked about marrying me. But then he terrified me with deliriously happy talk of living in some suburban house and having six babies one after the other. I hadn't even decided whether I wanted to someday have a boy, or be a boy.

I was in one of my disguise-yourself-as-a-boy phases. My short dark hair, lack of makeup, my loose sweatshirt and jeans created an image most teenage girls would not strive for. "Can I help you, sonny?" the storekeeper asked. I felt a sense of triumph tinged with guilt about my deceit whenever I succeeded in passing. I made my request: "The Sunday *Times*, please." The middle-aged man behind the counter looked embarrassed. I guess my voice was a giveaway. "I'm sorry," he said, "I thought you were a boy." That's the idea, I thought, you're supposed to think I'm a boy, and I'm sorry to have to do that to you, but I have to prove I can fool you, so don't apologize. This isn't very nice of me, you know, but it doesn't seem right to have to give up all the advantages of one sex in favor of the other's.

"No, you can't touch me there," I explained to my date. I was in the car with a seventeen-year-old boy I'd met at some dance. I'd now perfected the prostitute look: tight skirt, low-cut top, teased hair, and lots of makeup. I felt I should take responsibility for creating the wrong impression, so I continued to explain. "You know, I'm an honor student," I informed him, because serious girls weren't expected to have sex. "You? Are you kidding?" It was difficult to say what I was doing. The slut look offset the tomboy look, which offset the fact that I'd lost my father. He drove me home, disappointed.

At the Jewish Child Care Association headquarters they had a medical department. I loved going there for checkups, because I got to see Dr. Goldstein. Tall and husky, he was the nicest man in the world, and he was there almost every time I went. He had a way of taking children seriously, which many adults can't do. And he was even kinder to foster children than most pediatricians are to children with parents. He listened carefully and respectfully to everything I told him. He even seemed to believe me when I said I'd become a doctor someday. I was convinced he took me more seriously than I took myself. I liked the nurses, too, especially Miss Coburn.

They were always very happy to see me, and they treated me like I was someone important. Since they never found anything wrong with me, I thought of the visits as social calls.

But it was different when I went to a doctor on the outside. Sometimes they complained that they didn't get paid enough. Sometimes they were just plain mean. Once I had to go to a gynecologist for a pelvic examination because I had to urinate dozens of times a day, and even then still had the sensation of having to go to the bathroom. I was lying in the stirrups and he burst out laughing when I confirmed that I was a virgin. I had no idea why this was funny to him, but my sense of humiliation was intense. Another time, hoping that moving my prominent teeth back would help me stop believing I was ugly, I asked for braces, and the JCCA agreed to provide them. The orthodontist announced that he couldn't make me beautiful, but he'd do the best he could. Maybe the health care professionals willing to see foster children at reduced rates all had such terrible personalities that no one else would go to them. But there was no parent there to protect you—and anyway, you should be grateful that you got cared for at all. Be grateful that anyone took you in and fed and housed you. And the fact is I was grateful. Maybe in another time and place, I would have been left all alone to fend for myself. Feeling grateful helped mitigate my anger, and I learned to take nothing for granted.

Some people just don't like kids with no parents. Like Jenny's mother, whose daughter was the only girl in the class with a higher grade-point average than mine. Her two parents and brother looked completely identical with their square faces and full bodies, as if they'd been made using a plaster mold.

"My mother doesn't want me to play with you. She says you're a foster child." Oh, I thought, I guess that makes sense—in fact, it confirmed my theory: bad children lose their parents. I had no perspective on the terrible feelings of unworthiness that had become central to my view of myself. Since children love themselves to the extent they feel loved, and since I felt loved by no one, I'd lost all sense of valuing myself, except in one area: school, the one place I could still elicit the praise and admiration I so desperately wanted.

"What would you prefer, science or art?"

"I'll do science," I told Mr. Norris. My guidance counselor had taken an instant liking to me. He listened seriously as he helped me decide what courses I should be taking. He was the one who would ultimately insist I belonged in college. I was thinking of nursing school, I told him. It's only three years— no point in being dependent for as long as it takes to get through college and then still not have a trade when you're done. And I hear I can get a scholarship and live there. "That's not for you," he insisted. "You belong in college. After that, you can decide what's next." He wouldn't take no for an answer. It wasn't very often that anyone pursued me, or could see through my protests that I really wanted to be pursued. Most adults gave up right away.

When I turned sixteen, I took a job at Woolworth's. I worked twenty hours a week: every day after school and all day Saturday. I loved this job selling housewares and running the cash register. And I adored Ruth, who was very short and worked right next to me in the pet department. Her husband was twice as tall as she was, and he'd proposed to her on the first date! Ruth sold goldfish, parakeets, and canaries. I felt comfortable and useful in this place. No one cared who my parents were—they didn't even ask. I worked fast, fast, fast, and invented extra jobs for myself: I ran the freight elevator up to the stockroom, where I rummaged around for more glassware to create new and prettier displays; I raced to wash dishes at the soda fountain when it got busy; I served as the final arbiter in mathematical disputes between customers and salespeople. Now I'd found something else that, like school, helped me forget my circumstances: work!

I walk to the stretcher to see my new admission, and I pick up her chart. Twenty-year-old single black female, fever 104 degrees, diagnosis pyelonephritis. She's in agony from the pain of her kidney infection, and she looks terrible. The nursing staff have gotten her into bed, and I take her history. What did your father die of? In a car accident. I was a baby. What did your mother die of? Cancer. I was three. These are routine questions, but these are not the routine answers. What happened then? A long series of homes and placements. Have you ever had a kidney infection before? All the time. I had cancer of the uterus when I was six. They removed it and gave me radiation. She goes on to explain that the radiation scarred her bladder. She could no longer urinate normally. So they attached the tubes from her kidneys, the ureters, to a piece of bowel, which then exited her abdomen, where it connected to a plastic bag that collected her urine. Unfortunately, this unnatural form of human plumbing leaves her vulnerable to kidney infections, and she gets them all the time.

I'm writing all this down in her chart as if she were telling me a perfectly reasonable and ordinary story. She had lost both her parents and her own health by the time she was six years old. I examine her, but when I start to perform the routine pelvic exam, she winces at the slightest touch of her vagina. The radiation has scarred her there, too. And you mean you can't have sex, either, I'm thinking, trying to imagine how she handles this additional blow as well. I think of my own suffering over much less, and I try to imagine how she survives at all. But I can't. Don't worry, I say to her, we'll get you started on an intravenous antibiotic right away.

She gets better fast, amazingly so, and goes home in a week. The next week, she shows up for an outpatient appointment and I barely recognize her. She looks beautiful, vibrant, dressed in stylish clothes, giggling with her coworkers from the telephone company who have accompanied her to the appointment. I feel pleased and relieved. Good for you! Keep it up! She has a life, in spite of it all. She can work, be productive, make money, be independent, and have coworkers who cheer her on. She and I have both learned this: work makes you part of the world.

After I got my job at Woolworth's, I spent less time at home and made my own money, so I didn't have to nag Erma and we fought less. Still another turning point occurred when, after years of discontent over how I looked, I had a dramatic insight into my problem. I had felt ugly ever since my mother died. I criticized each part of my body in turn: it started with my hair sticking up in bumps. After that, my breasts pointed the wrong way, then my legs were too fat, soon my freckles were too dark, now my behind was misshapen, next my hair was the wrong color. But it finally struck me with great clarity: the real problem was my indented chin! And thus arose my "chin theory": I was excited to tell my sister, who looked just like me.

There are two kinds of people in the world: those with chins that protrude and those with chins that recede. Ours are the much less desirable receding kind. This, I assured my sister, explains it all, explains why we've been abandoned to this fate. Of course, this theory was our secret, and we never let anyone else know.

I felt closer to my sister. At seventeen, I had solved the mystery that had plagued us all these years. My mood improved and some of my humor returned. After all, my chin was bad, but I had secretly concluded that hers was even worse, and that I'd won this all-important contest. We regularly stared in the mirror, carefully examining our profiles to fully delineate the extent of the problem. We took pictures of ourselves in photo booths so that we could make even more detailed analyses. Other times, we ventured into the streets of Lynbrook on a campaign to discover who had a proper chin and who did not. We walked into town, spotting both kinds of people, expressing admiration for those with the right kind of chins, and pity for those who, like us, were missing them. Our most remarkable encounter occurred in the shoe store. We could not get over it—an astounding sight. The salesman went to fetch our shoes and we whispered and giggled over the state of his chin. Had we ever seen a more severe case? Where his chin should have been, there was a tremendous indentation. It could be worse, we realized. We could have chins like that. With my new job, and my new chin theory, I started to feel better. I still felt the shame of being so visibly parentless, but now I'd focused on a single defect shared by others even less fortunate than me. My acute misery became only a dull ache, and my state of detachment a familiar companion.

———

I could not describe my feelings in words, so my body became the center of my anxieties. Narrowing it down to my chin worked for a while, but during my senior year in high school I developed a new symptom: I was up every night until two in the morning. I wanted to think it was because I had so much to do, working at Woolworth's every day, perfecting my schoolwork so I could keep getting all those A's, but I suspected this was not the explanation. I was short of breath almost all the time, and I feared that if I closed my eyes and fell asleep, I would stop breathing completely. Or maybe the lump in my throat would make me choke and suffocate. I'd been to this doctor and that one, and they all told me there was nothing wrong, so maybe, I thought, it was all in my head. But my doubts were persistent. I was convinced I had become my dying mother.

I won't discover until I am a third-year medical student that there is a real illness for every frightening invention of my imagination. I don't notice anything visibly wrong with the two-year-old girl the pediatrician is holding in his arms. Yet she's never lived anywhere except Bellevue Hospital. "Ondine's Curse," the pediatrician explains to us third-year medical students, using an informal term for a form of sleep apnea. "If she falls asleep, she stops breathing. So she lives here, and we keep her on a respirator whenever she takes a nap or goes to sleep at night. I think of the vast difference between this little girl's physical struggle to breathe and my own psychological trouble, but I will become a psychiatrist before I learn that what I had was anxiety, a real affliction with real physical symptoms, and not, as was commonly believed at the time, "just in your head."

It was a fight between fear and exhaustion every night before I succumbed to half a night's sleep. I would be so tired in the morning that I would just turn off the alarm and go right back to sleep until someone ran upstairs to wake us. Seeing what time it was, I'd panic. If I missed school, if I failed to get those perfect grades, I'd have nothing to hold on to. I had to run around in a frenzy to get ready and get out. My solution was to buy five alarm clocks, set them sequentially a few minutes apart, and then place them in different locations in the room. I had to get up to shut off each one in turn, and by the time I got to the last one, I was awake.

When it came time to apply to college, the Jewish Child Care Association made it very easy: I could go either to a tuition-free city college or to none at all. "But what if I get a scholarship?" Irrelevant. If a student didn't do well, she could lose the scholarship, and the JCCA didn't have any money for tuition, only living expenses. I was disappointed, but only briefly. I feared I wouldn't fit in at a fancy private college anyway. It was easier to stay where I belonged.

The City College of New York is located in the heart of Harlem, and I paid thirty-seven dollars a semester to go there. I attended school with ten thousand other freshmen, every one of them a commuter because there were no dorms. It was an hour and a half one way from Lynbrook on the Long Island Rail Road and the subway, but I liked the ride, ideal for homework, three hours of gentle rocking motion, with the hum of voices in the background, soothing white noise. At CCNY, I was back in my milieu: the fast, dirty, diverse city.

But I had something now that sounded very sophisticated to me: a patron. Sarah Hoffman was a schoolteacher who gave money to the Jewish Child Care Association to send girls like me to college. I would have been able to go to college even if Sarah Hoffman hadn't given money, but when my social worker proposed the idea of having a patron, I accepted, since I guessed I needed one, whatever they did. In Sarah's case, it meant taking me out to concerts and dinners during which I toiled mightily to make intelligent and refined conversation.

Sarah lived on the seventeenth floor of a downtown Manhattan apartment building which had two elevators that stopped on alternate floors. This was a novel and amusing arrangement, except that the even-floors elevator always seemed to come first when of course I needed the odd-floors one. Her apartment was very neat, with lots of fancy-looking knickknacks, including a Tiffany lamp, which I knew was something only rich people owned. We got together every three months or so, and she would take me to real restaurants, the kind where they serve seafood in cream sauce sitting inside an actual seashell. Then we'd go off to concerts, something I viewed as an opportunity to extend my horizons, however boring I found the actual events. As we sat in the next to last row in one of the balconies of Carnegie Hall, Sarah told me what a great violinist we were about to hear. His name meant nothing to me, but I peered down at the stage from our stratospheric perch and there he was, sure enough, looking about the size of a grasshopper. He began to play, and I began to fall asleep, recovering in time to pinch myself awake and remind myself that only a philistine would sleep through such a special cultural event. My boredom persisted, concert after concert, so I took a music course one semester and bought a slew of classical records, setting them up on the record changer so they would drop down one after the other. I listened and listened until I finally found pleasure in the sweet melodies and the sounds of every instrument. In my mind, this was the first step in a transformation. I felt myself on the road to becoming cultured, a respectable member of the middle class, included in a larger world, something more than I used to be. Something more than an orphan.

Chapter 7

FATHER

(1964)

"Hi. My name is Francine Cournos. My father's name was Alexander. Did you know him?" My heart was pounding, worried that this stranger named John Cournos would greet my call as an unwelcome intrusion. This would be a moment of truth. I'd never met any member of my father's family, but occasionally my Uncle Milton had mentioned that my father had a relative who was a writer. I had made some desultory efforts to track him down, aided by the fact that the name Cournos is conveniently distinctive: almost no one has it. In high school, I sometimes casually searched card cata-

logues and *Who's Who* directories. Every search for my surname led to this John Cournos and no other. Then I discovered he was listed in the Manhattan telephone book. It was
strange to think I might be related to a man who lived so close
by yet was completely disconnected from me. I liked to day-
dream about having such an interesting and intelligent long-
lost relative, but the prospect of contacting him made me
more anxious than hopeful, and considerable time passed
before I felt worldly and courageous enough to call.

I knew almost nothing about my father. My ignorance of
him and his life seemed on the one hand to make little difference. He had died and left me, and I wanted to believe he did-
n't count anymore, if he ever did—so why would I pursue him?
Yet there was an empty space in my memory where my father
belonged. "Yes," said the voice on the phone. "Alexander was
my brother." Just like that! One phone call and I had found
my father's brother!

I arranged to meet my Uncle John in his home in
Washington Square—what a perfectly romantic place for a
writer to live!—and I was looking forward to an afternoon in
a bohemian writer's Village apartment. But even given my
expectations, his living quarters astonished me. Two small
rooms plus a tiny kitchen with almost no furniture. Instead,
there were piles of paper, thigh-high, covering the entire floor
space, with tiny aisles between them for pedestrians to squeeze
through. So this is how a real writer lives!

He was seventy-eight years old when I met him, hunched
over but probably once tall, and still lanky. He had a full,
thick head of white hair above a broad forehead, brown eyes,
and an unapologetically large and sharp nose. The face certainly fit: literary, writerly, a face that would look perfect on
the back cover of a novel. He moved and walked like a frail

old man, but intellectually he was completely intact. He was a widower with one stepchild and lived here alone. He offered me black coffee with cognac, which I accepted even though I liked neither ingredient. I sipped politely while he explained himself. He was a novelist, a critic, a translator of Russian books, and a poet. He gave me his latest book of poems. His apartment belonged to New York University, and they wanted to evict him. But he was not going anywhere, ever. How could he, I thought, looking around at the mounds of paper arranged in a way that only he could comprehend. How could they possibly move all this stuff without destroying his filing system?

"What do you do?" he finally asked.

"I'm a freshman at City College," I told him. "I study chemistry."

"Chemistry?" John didn't like chemistry. In fact, he didn't think much of science in general—he claimed it was useless and interfered with the flowering of the human spirit. I worried that this meant he didn't think much of me, either. Although I was excited to find John, a genuine relative, I couldn't help noticing how little this translated into any feeling of connection between us. We chatted further, I reluctantly swallowed the rest of my cognac-laced coffee, and it seemed time to leave. "And by the way," he added just before I departed, "your Aunt Lydia has a daughter who's coming to New York soon, and I'm going to tell her to call you and meet you." Uncle John was as good as his word: two weeks later I got a call from my cousin Dorothy, who was staying at the Hilton Hotel in Manhattan. We arranged to meet. Of course, I brought Alexis along with me.

We showed up at the appointed hour. I was nervous, but Dorothy immediately put us at ease. She was a small, thin woman in her late fifties, a professor, she told us, at a college in Phoenix. We went to a restaurant for lunch, and sat at a cozy table, Dorothy on one side, Alexis and I on the other. Dorothy was very articulate, lively, and enthusiastic in expressing her delight at discovering us. But the same fog that separated me from John still hung in the air, and I couldn't make the encounter seem real. This woman is my relative? But she's a total stranger. I can see how animated she is, but I can't figure out why. She doesn't even know me. I imagined that she must be rich, coming all the way here from Arizona, staying in a fancy hotel, and then flying off to Europe. The longest trip I'd ever taken in my life was to New Jersey. What could we possibly have in common? I listened to her words and I watched her gestures, but I felt more like an objective observer of an alien being than a participant in the give-and-take of conversation. I liked her, but I couldn't overcome the sensation that she, and the entire group of people she was so eagerly describing to us, were only strangers. Since I barely saw the relatives I did know, did I need more whom I'd never even met? I had no idea that such a relationship could be built from scratch, and when I didn't feel an instant connection, I was disappointed.

After our meeting, we began exchanging letters. Hers were very inviting: "I was delighted to hear from you. . . . I want to become better acquainted with you and Alexis, my only girl cousins. For eons, I was the only female offspring in the family, on either side. And now I find you, flesh and blood, kith and kin, and I like it—very much! We will have the chance to become really acquainted next summer. I wish you weren't so far away."

Most important, Dorothy, unlike Uncle John, had a lot to say about my father. "I cannot locate any picture of your father," she wrote. "He was camera-shy, my mother tells me. When I was a little girl, and on through my teens, he spent countless hours telling me fascinating and little-known things about well-known and little-known things. His knowledge seemed to me infinite, and I needn't tell you that he was my favorite uncle. He always helped with my algebra and geometry, in which I had no interest at all. He was a very gentle, lovable man, with great strength of character and unbelievable moral stamina, courageous beyond description, and uncompromising and unshakable when it came to matters of his conviction and integrity. Both of you girls can be proud, indeed, of your heritage and background. All your father's brothers and sisters were unusually talented, both in the sciences and the arts . . . and their forebears were intellectuals from way back."

Dorothy also sent me a picture of herself with her mother, my Aunt Lydia, and several boxes of fancy secondhand clothes that I could alter on Erma's sewing machine so they'd fit perfectly. I was glad that Dorothy had an interest in me, and that she had such wonderful things to say about my father. I'd always believed that he was everything Dorothy now said he was, and more, since it was easy to have a perfect father when you had no memories to suggest otherwise. But if everything she said was true, then at the same time I wanted to avoid hearing it, because it seemed too painful to think about all I had missed out on—a father who was kind and gentle, and who would have taught me many fascinating and little-known things, who would have been here to rescue me when Mom's family didn't want me anymore. I just couldn't make it across the gulf that separated me from a past I'd given up on. He left me, my father, a deserter. He no longer mattered. I felt as if I would just as soon rebury what I had unearthed. My correspondence with Dorothy became intermittent, then died.

I continued to see Uncle John occasionally. It was easier
with him. He never pursued me, never called, and had no
expectations of becoming close. His lack of feeling fit well
with my own need to keep my distance, so I called and visited Uncle John from time to time over the remaining four
years of his life.

"I found something," John announced one day, rummaging
through the papers on his desk. "Yes, here it is." He handed
me three yellowed pages, a carbon copy of a letter my father
had written to their mother. I took the papers from his hand,
and this document, this chance to hear my father speak in his
own words, this irresistible opportunity to form my own idea
of him, gripped and held my attention, thrilled me as meeting
with his relatives never had. John then told me that my father
had been in prison for pursuing political activities to which
the rest of the family was unsympathetic, and the result had
been the opening of a rift between them that never closed.
Eventually, they lost all contact with him. What did it mean
to have a father who had been in prison? What kind of political activities had he been involved in?

I read and reread my father's letter, looking for clues. The
yellowed paper was dated "July 4, 1923"—twenty years before
he married my mother. "Leavenworth, Kansas" read the line
under the date. "Dearest Mother," the letter began. That
sounded formal, and intelligent. "It grieves me to think . . ."—
and here the letter picked up in the middle of some ongoing
conversation, as my father explained that he was not trying to
prolong his prison stay by refusing to recant some principle or
belief. But why was he in prison? The letter hinted that it was
a very public matter: "Campaigns on our behalf . . . Senator
Reffer's report . . . This matter will be brought up before
Congress. . . ." What matter? "I may in conclusion say that I

am not taking this stand because I personally prefer my own happiness to yours. . . . But there are other things besides personal happiness." He's so right about that. I've learned that, too. See? We think alike! "If you exclude the pain I feel because of your unhappiness, I am blessed with excellent health and a nature such as cannot help but extract a good deal of happiness no matter what the situation. . . . Have faith, and you will find your faith justified." Dad, I don't really know you, or even remember you very much, but I can see that I'm your daughter. Prison is much more difficult than my own situation, but I know what you mean about seeking the positive in the face of adversity. The letter ended, "This agitation not being confined to radical papers, but also being expressed in big daily articles . . . leads me to think the matter will wind up as after the Civil War. Your loving son, Alex."

Determined to decode my father's letter, I went to the New York Public Library on Forty-second Street to search through microfilms of the *New York Times*, working my way backward and forward in time from July 4, 1923. I examined hundreds of pages, an inefficient research method that perfectly suited my obsessive desire to disappear into a world of written words in the pursuit of some tangible truth. And I found it! Alexander Cournos, member of the Industrial Workers of the World, sentenced to ten years in prison in 1918, then pardoned in 1923. My father was a member of the Wobblies, the labor group whose aim was to organize all the world's workers into "One Big Union." He was arrested in 1917, along with more than one hundred others, for trying to organize workers into unions, an act that certain politicians and prosecutors viewed as seditious interference with the production of war matériel. I learned that the Wobblies pioneered the labor-organizing techniques that would later be used more successfully by the American Federation of Labor and the Congress of Industrial Organizations. I felt a mixture of pride and concern about his past, and I wondered how it might reflect on me. A little knowledge was all I could tolerate for the moment, and I went no further in my research. I held on to the positive image: I now knew that my father believed deeply in a cause, that he had a fighting spirit. Over the years, I would feel him watching over me whenever I needed to defend my own beliefs, and I tried to live up to what I imagined he would have expected of me. My father and his intellectually accomplished family were a model of how to be in the world, but as for being loved by them, no, they were too far away. For that, I turned to others.

Chapter 8

LEAVING AGAIN

(1964–1967)

Among foster children, I was one of the lucky ones. For most, the money runs out when they turn eighteen. The child is "emancipated," as if parentless children at eighteen have suddenly acquired the skills to live as independent adults. Once when I was in the tiny waiting room of the medical department at JCCA headquarters, I met three fair-haired teenage girls. I was surprised by the shiny gold crosses hanging on chains from their necks. Except for my own foster family, I had hardly spoken to other foster children, nor ever met one my own age. We started to talk. They were Irish Catholic, they told me, but they never explained why they'd come to a Jewish agency for a medical exam. They'd soon turn eighteen, leave their foster homes, and be on their own. "Doing what?" I asked, but none of them could say. I could see their anxiety—I could feel it. I was lucky to have been born a Jew, I was thinking, because the JCCA had agreed to support me through college. Of course, even if they hadn't, Erma would never have kicked me out—as it later became evident, she would never kick any of her foster children out, even when the money had dried up. I couldn't leave home by going away to college, because here I was, happily commuting to what for all practical purposes could be grade 13 of high school. Instead, I got to leave in a more typical teenage way—after a fight over my boyfriend.

The trouble began during my second semester, when I decided to work for the City College engineering newspaper. The managing editor was a senior. Six feet two, heavyset, big nose, dark hair, dark eyes, he carried himself with great authority, and pursued me with a determination that suggested resistance was pointless. I was not even sure I liked him, but I was mesmerized by the intensity of his quest, by his declarations of love, by his patient insistence. In tiny steps, over many months, we became lovers, and I'd never been so on fire. Late at night, we made love in his father's deserted clothing store, neatly removing the softest coats and dresses from their hangers and spreading them on the floor. The delicious smell of fresh bread and cake being made in the bakery next door wafted into the room. The smells and the softness and the lovemaking stirred in me a feeling of such exquisite pleasure that I knew it was worth it, worth having survived no matter what I had lost.

One morning, during one of my many arguments with Erma

over getting home too late, she announced that if I didn't like it here, I could just leave. But this was not the angry and empty rhetorical suggestion it might have been in someone else's mother-daughter argument: in my case, I really could move out. My stipend for room and board at college would follow me wherever I lived. So that very day, on the Upper West Side of Manhattan, I rented a room from an old lady who shared her huge, old-fashioned six-room apartment with two boarders and seven cats. Over the next eight years I would live in six other Manhattan apartments, with varying combinations of roommates, a slew of gray and black cats, tanks of tropical fish, and a mouse-eating python, before I finally settled back down in the Bronx. But for now, this place would do. That night, I came home and made my announcement: I'm leaving, just like you told me to. Erma was terribly hurt—and good and mad, too. Only a year ago she had built a beautiful new room for me over the garage. She couldn't believe I could be so ungrateful. Alexis felt bad, too—in her eyes, I was deserting her as well. But I was not thinking of her, or really much of Erma. All that was overshadowed by my sexual passion.

And besides, I had to escape. I had been numb for too long, and my intense desire for a man awakened me. To want something so passionately seemed to counter the frightening moments when, lying alone in bed in my rented room, feeling that if I died it might be days before anyone would even notice, I tried to imagine what death was like, what it meant not to exist, to have the world disappear and become nothing, only to discover that my connection to life was still sustained by the hope of finding enduring love.

Unfortunately, I was able only to re-create new versions of familiar and painful relationships. After two years of great passion, my boyfriend started to unravel. I was unable to recognize his emerging mental illness, perhaps the result of the steroids he'd started taking to treat a case of inflammatory bowel disease that he'd had since childhood. But I didn't need a rational explanation for his erratic behavior, since I knew that sooner or later everyone deserted me. That truth seemed more central to my life than any realistic assessment of what was actually happening. "You're controlling my mind, like a computer," he said menacingly, and as the months passed, his paranoia grew, his rage mounted, and his love evaporated. At night I had a recurrent dream of being chased through the subway by a man with a knife. By day I professed my innocence, but it did no good. When I got really upset, I could make him disappear by picking up my chemistry books and starting to study—I still had to get those A's, and I was capable of focusing entirely on that no matter what else was going on. But this only made him even more furious, and one day I got so scared by his angry attacks that I had to escape.

"I'm very upset and I need to come home tomorrow." Erma said not to wait but to come right now, so I took the evening train back to Lynbrook. It felt safe, riding away from the city, arriving back in Lynbrook, no questions asked about my lunatic boyfriend even though it was for him that I'd left in the first place. I sat in the kitchen where Erma served me plates of food and Esther kept me company, staring at me with such tenderness and concern that I was reminded of who I once was when I was capable of such empathy for my dying mother.

In the end, it was my relationship with Erma that survived. Our refusal to speak only lasted for a few months after my departure. Then Erma sent me a note demanding money for my share of some unpaid phone bill, but by now I'd grown smarter, so I took it as an invitation. I sent the money with a polite note, and then she responded with a friendly phone call, and before we knew it, we were together again and I was making regular visits home to catch up with Alexis and David and Esther, and to get to know my little foster brother Alan. Erma and I never became intimate—we didn't trust each other with our feelings enough to do that—but I learned the value of our enduring commitment, of the structure that commitment provided, and of the security of having a home base long after the foster care agency was no longer involved in my care.

Fortified by my stay with Erma, I returned to the city. My boyfriend and I had broken up so many times it was impossible to say who really ended the relationship. But it hardly mattered, since the entire experience mystified me. First a man loved me, then he hated me; I was a lost soul, claimed then discarded. I had no idea who this man really was, or how I had stumbled into a relationship that was so punishing. In the end, I felt devastated, which only proved my point: men seduce and abandon you, and no relationship can last. My own role eluded me, buried in anger and disappointment and fear that I was very far from acknowledging.

Later, when I am a psychiatrist doing couples therapy, I will discover for myself the absolutely uncanny ability of people to find partners who allow them to reexperience the unhappy love relationships of childhood. "How could that be?" one couple once asked me, bewildered that although they had hardly known each other when they fell in love, both had nevertheless selected a perfect match, allowing them to reenact their emotional history. The phenomenon remains astonishing no matter how many times I see it.

But it was not my problems with men that finally landed me in therapy, or at least that was not what I was thinking about when I had my first encounter. The psychiatrist, a short, talkative middle-aged brunette, looked me up and down. "You have a nice body," she said. "I can see why men would ask you out." That's a pretty weird statement, I was thinking. At twenty-one, I had unintentionally convinced the Jewish Child Care Association that I needed therapy. When I was nineteen, I had inquired about psychotherapy but instead got a prescription for Miltown, at the time a very popular antianxiety drug. I took it infrequently, but I liked the reassurance of carrying it around in my purse, available for emergencies. Finally, after two years, the bottle ran out, and in a moment of panic I called to ask for another prescription. When I had asked for a psychiatrist two years earlier, they had given me pills. Now I asked for pills and they gave me a psychiatrist. Go figure.

Maybe this time my panic was more apparent. I'd been sitting in front of the engineering building at City College eating a sandwich, still forlorn about the end of my first love affair, when I started to choke on the bread. My only thought between gasps for breath was: I'm going to die—just like my mother. I'm going to suffocate.

I was recounting my story to the psychiatrist. It was a relief to tell someone about how an event as trivial as lunch could strike such terror in my heart. I didn't know much about psychology, but I was thinking, This is a little crazy, and a psychiatrist is someone who understands what's crazy. I told her all about my mother, her cancer, my hypochondria, my constant fear of dying, my visits to numerous medical doctors for every pain or lump that I was sure was the beginning of the end. The reassurance lasted for a few days, I explained, but then the fear would return, and it all seemed so real, like I really was going to die.

She pulled out a pad of lined paper and drew two diagrams, one of the male orgasm and one of the female. She wanted to let me know the all-important difference. The male orgasm peaks much more rapidly, she showed me with the sharp rise and fall of her graph, whereas the female orgasm occurs more slowly and is more prolonged. I'm in a panic because I'm going to die, and this woman is drawing me freehand graphs of orgasms!

I tried to explain that the physiology of the human orgasm was not relevant to my problem. Sex, I told her, is probably the only problem I don't have—I'm quite good at that. But I could see she wasn't buying it. When our forty-five minutes were up, she announced that her next patient had canceled and that she was prepared to spend another forty-five minutes with me. That's when she began to comment on my body. I wondered if she was coming on to me, but then totally dismissed the thought as even more insane than my original complaint. It was a relief when the ninety minutes came to an end. This cure was worse than the disease. The encounter seemed yet another of the strange or incomprehensible or frightening things that adults in authority always seemed to do. But I did have some self-protective instincts.

"I'm not going back to her," I told my Austrian social worker. "She's even crazier than me."

"I'll explain you don't want to see a woman," she told me. "I'll ask for a man." And I was amazed when she actually produced one for me. There was nothing seductive about this one, and all of his questions were pointed and relevant, sometimes uncomfortably so.

"Who are you closest to?" he asked. I was stumped. Not a

single person came to mind. How could I admit to that? He'd think there was really something wrong with me, not just that I had irrational fears of choking to death.

"Gene, my boyfriend." Here I was, back to the subject of men again. Gene was a pot-smoking trumpet player with a little black goatee, and I'd been seeing him for exactly one week to the day, but this seemed like a sensible answer, appropriate for a twenty-one-year-old college student.

"How long have you known Gene?" He had to ask that. If I said one week, he'd surely think I was completely lacking in human connections.

"One month" popped out, as if this made a big difference. And for the rest of my year and a half in treatment, I remembered to always backdate meeting Gene by those critical three weeks. He concluded the initial visit: "And remember, therapy isn't a reason for staying alive."

"Don't worry," I informed him, "I haven't ever been suicidal." You asshole, I continued in my head, how do you think I stayed alive all these years until you came along? I'm not so pathetic that I need *you* as the center of my universe.

I'd used up my options—there were no genders left. Which was worse, an intrusive, sexually preoccupied woman or a smart, distant, arrogant man? No contest: I'd pick distance any day.

My therapist was Italian, but he was nothing like my mother's boyfriend Sam. He was young and wore elegant suits and fancy shoes, and his cigarettes had filters. He stared at me impassively while I spoke, and then, when he had something to say, talked in long, intelligent paragraphs with just enough of an Italian accent to sound very sophisticated. His office was on the second floor of a hospital for adolescents who looked like they were under the spell of some powerful drugs, and I could only wonder how far away I was (or my crazy ex-boyfriend was) from living in this place, too. I liked having someone to talk to, someone remote and therefore safe, yet also smart and attentive. I stored up lots to say every Tuesday and Thursday, and the words gave shape to my otherwise utterly confused attempts to become close to others.

I began to see that my halfhearted search for Dad and my haphazard choices of men and the sexual drive that convinced me I was still part of life, and my terror of choking and dying like Mom, and my appreciative but detached relationship to Erma were all part of the same maddening struggle between two warring parts of me. One side insisted on managing without being close to anyone, said it's just not worth it, people are too unreliable, only a fool would persist in the face of all the evidence that it never works out and never will. But the other part of me was desperate, needy, driven by desire, afraid to be alone. I hated my contradictory feelings and wished I could banish them, but there was no escape.

I was sitting in a lawyer's office, an appearance requested in one of Uncle Milton's rare telephone calls. I never knew it, but apparently I was an heiress: my mother had left me an insurance policy worth $3,000, and now that I was twenty-one and a responsible adult, Milton, my guardian, was obliged to turn over the money to me.

Uncle Milton liked to say this: "If you ever need anything, don't hesitate to call." Once I took him up on the offer. I was nineteen years old, but you had to be twenty-one to sign the $88-a-month lease on the apartment I'd just found with another City College student. I needed an adult to co-sign, so

I called Uncle Milton to ask him. He categorically refused. He couldn't take on such a financial risk, he said, it was just impossible. "I have my own family to think about," he explained. Uncle Milton had made it vividly clear yet again: I was not part of his family. The grotesque conclusion to our conversation: "And remember," Milton repeated, as if by rote, "if you ever need anything, don't hesitate to call." I asked my Austrian social worker to sign, I lent her my pen, and the apartment was mine.

But this time Milton had called me. The lawyer began with a long disquisition on Milton's virtues. The estimable Milton had watched over this money—all three thousand dollars of it—for ten years! He hadn't stolen a penny! The lawyer handed me the bank book containing the proceeds of my mother's life insurance policy. It was not much, but I was not sure I wanted any money at all, because it horrified me to think I had thus profited from my mother's death. "And here," Milton said, handing me a copy of the letter Mom wrote to Alexis and me shortly before she died.

I had seen this letter before, just after Mom's death, but I had no copy of it, and I had forgotten all about it. Now it came rushing back: not the contents of the letter itself but my horror at imagining my mother anticipating her own death, consciously facing the end of everything. The very thing we had refused to talk about she had silently put down on paper, knowing I would one day read it. I shivered, and now I remembered one sentence from the letter, the one it began with: "When you read this, I will be dead." That unforgettable sentence stood out crystal clear in my memory.

I brought the letter home, read it, and reread it. With each rereading, I hated it more. It didn't begin at all the way I remembered it. It was dated June 12, 1956. "I am terribly sorry that Fate has ordained my leaving you so soon." Why is she being so cool, so formal? "Try your best not to take it too badly," it blandly suggests. Not take it too badly? Are you kidding? It nearly destroyed me! "None of us have any control over these things." Another empty, useless platitude. "I want you to know that I have always loved you both very much." I don't believe it. You must have hated us to have left us like this. "Please try to get along harmoniously, and practice the principle of compromise . . . bickering and arguing over little things all the time only brings about hard feelings and unhappiness. . . ." Who are you talking to, Mom? Did you imagine we would forever remain little girls, arguing over toys? I'm not a little girl anymore: I'm Alexis's inept mother. I hate her, take care of her, and compete with her in a nearly insane fusion of conflicting feelings. "I have named as the executor of my estate your Uncle Milton . . . you can rest assured that you have a real and honest friend . . . the same is also true for the rest of the family." What family are you talking about? Milton is a pathetic fool, frightened of the world, concerned only with himself, barely capable of fulfilling even ordinary adult responsibilities, much less finding anything left over to offer us. And the rest of the family is no better. Surely, Mom, you don't actually believe what you've written here. "I am terribly sorry that I have been compelled to make things so difficult for you." At last, something that rings true, the only accurate thing you've said so far. "I hope you will both live very long, happy and healthy lives and that all your wishes may come true." Then why did you abandon us to people who only conspired to get rid of us? Far from wanting things to turn out well, you must have wanted to punish us.

I stared at the letter in my hands, hating it. It said nothing of use. That phrase I recollected so vividly—"When you read this, I will be dead"—appeared nowhere in the letter. This shocked me—I recalled it so distinctly. I put the letter away and did my best to forget all about it. My mother knew exactly what was happening, faced it squarely, but then persistently hid it from me. I had invented a sentence that encapsulated this realization, and it was for me the only important thing. In the end, rediscovering her letter was disappointing, only another reminder that memory is fragile, and that much of what we remember stems from the power of our emotional responses, those bright lights glowing against the dim background of the facts.

Chapter 9

DO NO HARM

(1967–1972)

Erma was listening on the other end of the phone. I had surprised myself by calling her to discuss something important. I'd never talked to my own mother about my worries, and I felt much closer to her, so this was a bit of an experiment. It was finally time to act on my plan, but I was wavering. I was between boyfriends, and I'd taken it into my head that I had a choice: to be a doctor or to be a wife. One or the other. I had already mentioned becoming a doctor to my grandmother and some of my aunts and uncles. When they wondered aloud why I would want to do something so depressing, I decided not to discuss the matter further with them.

I'd already passed the famous City College Cadaver Test, which required signing up for a trip to the New York City Medical Examiner's Office, where every violent or suspicious death in the city was investigated. Eight hard stone tables in one huge room, each equipped with a sink for draining fluids and a scale to weigh body parts. On each lay a dead body. The room next door was a giant walk-in refrigerator filled with what appeared to be filing cabinets. In each drawer, yet another body. "Look," one of the pathologists instructed us, sliding out a drawer. Inside lay the body of a man. His pale white skin was flaked; his swollen purple feet had large bulbous growths on them. "Homeless guy. Died of hypothermia. Froze to death." My mind was reeling, trying to orient itself in this surreal world where people froze to death and were then stored in filing cabinets. We watched a dissection. Slice the scalp, peel back the skin. Saw neatly through the skull with a little electric buzz saw. Remove the top, and there's the brain. Take a look. Move to the side of the table. One smooth silent slice with a sharp knife and the abdomen is open, the smell of fresh human bowel nauseating, overwhelming. But I didn't faint, and at City this meant you had the right stuff! Still I was afraid. "Maybe no man will ever love me if I become a doctor, and when I finish, I'll be four years older and all alone."

"Why wouldn't a man love you if you became a doctor?" Erma asked. "Anyway, you're not involved with a man now, so what are you going to do? Wait around for one? Believe me, the four years will pass no matter what you do, but if you spend the time in medical school, you'll be a doctor at the end."

There was comfort for me in Erma's commonsensical approach, and her logic was unassailable—at the end of four years, whatever else I did and whatever else happened, it was an absolute certainty that I would be four years older. With

Erma's help, I decided I could do it, and I made the decision rather late in the game, but in time to apply to medical school.

"Do you plan to marry and have a family?" The question came from one of the four male doctors simultaneously interviewing me for admission to Cornell Medical School.

"Yes. I hope to."

"So how will you balance being a doctor and having a family?" The question, of course, was meant to be rhetorical.

"Do you have a family?" I asked. My behavior was completely irrational under the circumstances, but I had decided to set him up for the kill.

"Yes."

"Then you tell me. How do you balance the two?"

A nice snotty answer, exactly the wrong tone for a medical school interview, but I couldn't help myself. I've just blown my chances of ever being admitted here, I thought, and yet I couldn't seem to find it in myself to feel regretful. The interview went on, but the high point had clearly passed. Finally, I was told I would be placed on the waiting list. "We've already filled our quota of six women," one of them helpfully explained.

In the end, I was accepted by New York University. In the 1960s, the best Jewish students from City College who applied to Manhattan's medical schools, no matter how good their college records and test scores, wound up at NYU. So much was this so that we (among ourselves only, and quietly) referred to our alma mater as NY Jew.

On the first day of medical school, we were assigned our cadavers in gross anatomy class. My three male compatriots and I named ours Julius because we all agreed that the name seemed sufficiently dignified for the tall, handsome, muscular man, skin the color of café au lait, lying on the cold stone slab. Most of the cadavers were unclaimed bodies that would otherwise have been buried in unmarked graves. Sometimes, as we were working, I silently talked to Julius, thanking him for the opportunity to discover what was really inside the human body and asking him about what had happened in his life to land him here, a victim of the lonely fate I myself feared so much.

I was trying hard not to end up like my cadaver. Toward the end of college, my Italian therapist suggested I apply for psychoanalysis. Maybe he thought two sessions a week were not enough for a case like mine, or that I had so much to say that I'd surely want to come four times. Maybe he was just trying to get rid of me. Yes, that was probably it. The JCCA had stopped paying for my therapy and I was using my little inheritance, but even at his reduced fee, I'd soon run out. And what would he do with me then, some poor soul he thinks is depending on him just to stay alive. I was not going to outstay my welcome this time, so I embarked on the process of finding a new treatment.

I had a less than clear idea of what psychoanalysis was, although I had read Freud's *Introductory Lectures*. I applied to three different institutes in New York City that specialized in training psychiatrists to become psychoanalysts—if you got into one of these, you worked with an analyst-in-training, and you only had to pay between fifty cents and two dollars a session, just about the amount I could afford. "You have to be disturbed just the right amount—not too much and not too little—to get accepted" was what I'd heard from one of my college friends. I wrote three long explanations of what I imagined to be my troubles, and underwent six interviews, not all of which were particularly pleasant. The one I liked least took place at the institution where my Italian therapist himself was still studying. I was in the middle of telling the interviewer an intimate story when a second psychoanalyst loudly knocked on the door, barged into the room, sat down, and glanced at me as if to say, "Just continue on while I voyeuristically listen in." I was relieved that I was coming to the end of the sex part of my story and was now heading on to the topic of my becoming a doctor. I talked on, trying to pretend that the intruder wasn't there.

But then the interloper spoke: "Suppose you're in analysis and your analyst decides you don't belong in medical school?"

Fuck you, was the first thought that entered my mind. Do you think I survive by caring what people think I should and shouldn't do? I'll do whatever I goddamn please. I responded in a tone that matched the intruder's hostility: "I'm sure that if in the course of analysis I discover I'm not suited to be a doctor, I'll decide for myself that I no longer want to pursue it." And if you don't like that answer, don't accept me, because no one tells me what to do! The intruder soon left. I tried to believe that the nice interviewer wasn't in on this, that he hadn't known a rude colleague would barge in and challenge me, that we were both victims. But I suspected that that wasn't the case, that this was a test I'd either passed or failed. I wanted to be admitted here—I was certainly in no position to pay for private treatment—and it surprised me that somehow I couldn't be diplomatic. When someone provoked me, I said whatever came to mind. I wasn't sure how a person who could hold her tongue so well in childhood had come by such a trait. Nor did I know then that this was only the beginning of what in full bloom would be the daring, outrageous part of my angry challenge to the world and especially to men in authority. I was relieved when the letter of acceptance came, but it was nearly a year before I was assigned to a student analyst.

Sitting in the waiting room of his Fifth Avenue office, I was taken aback when a tall, slender, startlingly handsome dark-haired man came out to introduce himself. What did they do? Assign me to a movie star? He invited me into his office. He was warm and friendly, and I started my story all over again.

"Why did they do that?" he asked during my second session.

"Do what?" I replied, even though I followed the question.

"You know, send you to a foster home. That's unusual, especially in a Jewish family, where people usually find a place for their own."

No one had ever asked me that question before, and he was the first person to suggest that something was wrong with them, not me. I was in equal measure moved by my analyst's sympathetic position and surprised by his willingness to articulate it.

I became intensely attached to my new therapist. His warmth and interest and insight were central to my hopes of building a new set of relationships to replace those I'd lost. But lying on a couch staring at the ceiling for forty-five minutes four times a week trying to say whatever came into my mind while another person sat behind me, out of sight—it all made me feel as if I'd entered some alternate universe, floating through murky space where nothing was quite real. Besides, who would say whatever comes to mind anyway? Certainly not me, cautious and controlled, suspicious and distrustful, ashamed and fearful. Just because I'd been accepted for psychoanalysis didn't mean I had to spread my inner life all over the place.

I never did learn to free-associate, and eventually he and I gave up the idea of formal psychoanalysis altogether and began to meet face-to-face. But this very maternal man (who in fact would make a career of studying babies) would help raise me, staying with me for eight years until I'd established a secure place in the adult world and was ready to be on my own.

Medical school was filled with cute guys—90 percent of the class was male. But as the first term began, I moved in with a chemistry graduate student I'd met during my last semester at City College. Men all around me, and still I thought I'd better settle on one fast. Between the first and second years of medical school, I married him. I had felt numb since adolescence, so I couldn't know if I was in love. But at twenty-three, I felt ancient, convinced there wouldn't be another chance. Someone had picked me out, and my persistent fear of being alone led me to accept the offer.

Fair-skinned with light brown hair, thin lips, and a reserved demeanor, my new husband was very scientific. He studied formulas, was never paranoid, and didn't smoke pot. He had a real family, too, not that I fit into it. His parents were German Jews who had come here long before World War II. His maternal grandmother lived with his parents. She was very old and very grouchy. She thought Eastern European Jews like me were inferior and ugly. I never realized that people believed there were inferior and superior Jews. Her own mother had died giving birth to her, and her father finished raising eight children all by himself. And then he got Parkinson's disease to boot. I guess that was enough to put my husband's grandmother in a permanent bad mood.

My in-laws were very religious, and they firmly believed that a woman's place was in the home. I was an atheist. I didn't like going to temple, and the only thing that really interested me was studying. I was completely unsuited to my new role: I didn't keep kosher, I didn't hand-wash the socks or bleach the graying undershirts, I didn't make proper dinners each containing a meat, a starch, and a vegetable. Really I was not good at this new role at all, and my failures led to fights and disappointment. He wanted me to be what I was not, and struggling to please him only interfered with the most important and satisfying moments in my life: studying. By the time medical school ended, we'd agreed to call it quits. I guess I should have married a man instead of a role, but I was too detached to know the difference. Yet I was starting to notice my feelings again, to sense the return of what had once seemed so natural, before the numbness enveloped me, before I gave up on being close to others.

At some point during medical school, most students develop a peculiar disorder: they become firmly convinced that they are about to die of whatever disease they just learned about. But I was ahead of the game. I arrived at medical school already afflicted. I was learning to hear through my stethoscope the characteristic "lub-dub" sound of the normal heart, the reliable template against which all abnormal sounds stand out. I decided to practice by listening to my own heart. Bad idea. I placed the stethoscope to my chest, and instead of hearing "lub-dub," I heard "lub-*swish*-dub," the characteristic sound of a systolic heart murmur. Terror engulfed me. I must have been born with congenital heart disease, or developed rheumatic fever after a strep throat, and it had left my heart's valves deformed. Or maybe I'd developed a brand-new disease. I'd been close to death many times—at least so I believed—and been reassured by doctors time and again. But this time there was something really wrong—I could hear it myself. I went to the Student Health Service, panicked.

"Yes," the doctor said. "I hear it. It's called an ejection murmur. That's a normal sound of blood flowing. Nothing at all." He looked at me, and unlike most, he saw my fear. "What else is wrong?" I blurted out my fear that surely one of the ever-present cysts in my breasts had become malignant and I would die, just like my mother. He examined me, talked to me, comforted me. His understanding and attentiveness were extraordinary, and I decided that he would be the one I would go to whenever I needed reassurance. Three months later, my new doctor, thirty-seven years old, was dead of a massive heart attack, leaving behind not only his admiring patients but also his wife and two small children. It made me overwhelmingly sad, and it profoundly offended my sense of fairness and justice. Student health was not the same without him.

As time passed, I was less frightened. The more I learned, the easier it was to make my own distinction between a healthy person and a dying one. I'd solved the mystery. I saw now that I was healthy. It was the person I was taking care of who was sick. In the end, at least in this sense, medical school reassured me.

He was seventeen, complaining of severe headaches. I peered into his right eye with my ophthalmoscope. It took some practice to learn to see the back of the eye, to become familiar with the red-tinted retina, the darker blood vessels that profuse it, the round white disk where the optic nerves from the brain connect to the back of the eye, making vision possible. I squinted, and searched, and then I saw it: a blurring of the usually sharp outline of the optic disk. I felt my heart beating. I was thrilled to see for the first time what I'd only read about in books. This was it: papilledema, the sure sign that pressure in the brain is too high, almost always an indication of something serious—and in a seventeen-year-old boy with headaches, probably a brain tumor. I looked at the left eye, and just as I suspected, the papilledema was there as well. But then I caught myself, horrified to be engrossed in a search for something that has gone wrong, something that another part of me hopes never to find. Later, when the diagnosis is confirmed, when I have the chance to get to know this young man and his bewildered mother, when he dies in a matter of months despite all our efforts, I feel frustrated, distraught, in mourning for my adolescent patient unjustly robbed of an adult life.

With each disease, there was an undeniable thrill in arriving at the right diagnosis, quickly followed by the pain of informing the victim, profound sorrow, and, inevitably, a sense of guilt that I found the morbid alluring. It was a compelling vice, this captivation that began when I was a child preoccupied with my mother's suffering and death, and yet, as my mastery of disease increased, my interest in it waned.

Four years of medical school, a year of internship, another

year of residency: six years of apprenticeship, and I now knew how to recognize the ailments nature imposes, and even the ones in which nature plays little role. I'd seen young victims of child abuse who had parts of their skulls removed to allow their swollen brains to expand while we waited to see if they would recover. I'd seen men with gruesome gunshot and knife wounds brought in under police guard, and I'd seen them get up, wrapped in bandages, and escape when the cop was momentarily distracted. I'd been whistled at by prisoners who had swallowed nails and razor blades wrapped in adhesive tape (largely harmless to the person who swallows them, but vivid on an X ray, where the tape cannot be seen)—the standard method of getting a vacation from prison by checking into the Bellevue Hospital prison ward. I'd had the eerie experience of listening to people predict the exact moment of their death and then watching them die on their self-imposed schedules. I'd seen old women in their final moments of life call for their long-gone mothers. Do the feelings of loss and longing ever go away?

"I'll give you a nickel if you let me die, girlie." The old man spoke to me as I admitted him to the Manhattan Veterans Administration Hospital. He'd been drinking for too many years, his liver had given way, his heart had stopped pumping right, and he was having trouble breathing. I declined his offer. Death was a defeat, and we didn't like losing. Seventeen days on a respirator, attached to intravenous lines, poked at and prodded, stuck with needles for daily diagnostic tests, the old soldier died anyway. I worried that our treatment was more like torture, and so it went time and again, a stream of people who had had enough, who were ready to die, whose only barrier now was their doctors' inability to call it quits. Years later, this would change radically when patients were expressly given the right to refuse heroic measures. This is of course a humane advance, and, looking back, I am shocked that we didn't implement it sooner. But I must admit that I am grateful that my own mother was never willing to give up, that she accepted every treatment no matter how painful or disfiguring, that she gave me every last day she could, that she never surrendered.

There were times when I was startled by my patients' emotional responses to grave illness. We admitted a forty-three-year-old man to the coronary care unit. He was young and vital, apparently healthy, but he had some atypical chest pain. His cardiogram was normal, but just to be on the safe side, we decided to monitor him. A few hours later, I was sitting in the nurses' station, watching his monitor, when the rhythmic line tracing his heartbeat suddenly went flat. I raced into his room just in time to see the last traces of consciousness fade from his face. Organized pandemonium ensued. We started pounding on his chest, pumping air into his lungs, injecting various medicines through an intravenous line, simultaneously wheeling the crash cart over to his bed. We turned on the defibrillator and slapped the paddles on his chest, delivering an electric shock to his heart through his chest wall. His body jerked and stiffened, then relaxed again onto the bed. One jolt, and it worked! His heart started beating, and consciousness quickly returned. He gazed around the room—at an impressive assemblage of anxious-looking nurses and doctors, electronic equipment, wires, paddles, syringes, strips of paper with tracings of his heartbeats, medicine vials spread all over the place—and what had just happened began to dawn on him. An expression of wonder and astonishment appeared on his face: he realized that he had just, quite literally, come back from the dead. We began to clean up, the cart was wheeled away, the crowd quietly dispersed. I was left alone with my patient. He had come out of a kind of Midsummer Night's Dream, enchanted with the first person he saw upon awakening. "You saved me," he announced. "Now I'm your slave."

I knew his assertion was ludicrous, but there it was. I was not really prepared for a slave, not at all. And maybe I couldn't handle my absurd attraction to the possibility that after all these years of doing without, a fatherly man would finally belong to me. I decided on the internist's last resort: I called in the psychiatrist, who worked his magic, carrying on some arcane conversation with the patient by the end of which the slave idea had disappeared. He was just my grateful patient again. How did the psychiatrist do this?

On another occasion, I was caring for a tall, dignified, seventy-five-year-old man in constant pain from prostate cancer that had spread to nearly every bone in his body. This overwhelming pain, I assumed, was the reason for his unexpected suicide attempt. As is routine in these situations, I called in the psychiatrist, who came up with a completely different explanation. My patient's sister had become seriously ill, but to spare him further suffering, the family had concealed the news from him. When he learned about his sister's illness accidentally through a friend, he concluded that the family had written him off—in his view, this refusal to inform him meant they considered him dead already, so why go on? When all this was uncovered, we brought in the family, who succeeded in reestablishing the trust that had been lost. Eight months later, readmitted for the last time, he died, surrounded by his family, knowing that he was included as one of them, to the very end. And again I wondered how this psychiatrist was able to talk with my patient about the painful feelings I found so intimidating.

It was a windy day in early March when a twenty-year-old man was brought into our emergency room, DOA, killed by a tree limb that snapped in the wind, fell on the back of his head, and broke his neck. I looked at him: young, normal, but now irretrievably lost. I called the family. Come quickly—there has been a serious accident. We'd been taught never to inform relatives about death over the phone, and it was a rule I never violated. His mom arrived. The supervising physician looked at me, and I stared back at him, my uneasiness beginning to blossom into fear. Was I to tell this terrified mother what had just happened to her son? I was enormously relieved when my supervisor, sensing my mounting dread, volunteered for the task himself. But this was of course not the solution; I couldn't remain the silent child forever frozen with panic. I tried harder to talk, to listen, to inquire for myself, and each time I succeeded, it was a small triumph.

I had once needed the Jewish Child Care Association, and now they apparently needed me. They asked me to speak at a fund-raising luncheon where I, along with three others, was to serve as an example to their contributors of how well the Jewish Federation had spent their money. I was appalled at the thought of being put on display, but the organization had been important to me, and I was determined to do what they wanted, even if it meant playing a role I found humiliating:

Young Woman Who, with Our Munificent Support, Has Overcome Adversity and Grown Up to Become a Doctor. At their suggestion, I arrived at the lunch dressed in my white hospital jacket and skirt, a stethoscope dangling from my pocket, doing my best to look the part. I hated the idea, but I felt obliged, even guilty: I owed them, and it was time to pay up.

I knew that I could just as well have felt proud, a foster child who had made good, who, with the financial help of these generous patrons, had fought the odds to become a successful person, a doctor no less. But as I gave my speech and told my story, I felt less like a competent adult professional than like a waif, a sad little orphan, my pitiful story put on display for complete strangers to contemplate. It was beginning to feel like that TV show "Queen for a Day"—you stand up and tell your heartrending story, and then they turn on the applause meter to determine whose tale is the most satisfyingly pathetic.

After the last of the four presenters had finished his story, one of the assembled philanthropists stood up: "I'll raise my contribution by $100,000." Others followed, with similarly remarkable pronouncements. Until I actually heard their names announced—Mr. and Mrs. This Department Store and Mr. and Mrs. That Department Store—it had never occurred to me that Macy's or Gimbel's or Bloomingdale's were all named for actual people. I thought they were just chic places to shop. By the end of the luncheon, the federation had raised $4.5 million. I left, my duty done, thoroughly ashamed of the circumstances that had made me such a fine fund-raiser.

I had been on call at the hospital for forty-eight hours. I probably should have stayed to confront the impossibility of my

childhood wish—that I could have saved my mother. I had
gone to medical school to bring her back to life. And here I
was, about to realize my plan to become a practicing doctor,
and the opportunity had presented itself. No patient came
closer than this one: dying just like my mother. Breast cancer
diffusely metastatic to her lungs, leaving behind a fifteen-year-
old son. I'd sat quietly by her bedside. I'd learned to do that
with every patient on the cancer ward. They almost always
talked. I know I'm dying, they'd say, but I don't want my family to know I know. And the family would say it the other way
around: Don't tell her it's fatal—she thinks she'll get better. It
was rare that they could tolerate talking openly. I understood
that. We had no tolerance at all. As if everything would go on
just like it was and never change. My sister will take care of
my son, my patient told me. I'd been giving her intravenous
Demerol—too much and too often, I feared—but that was the
only thing that calmed her. She was suffocating to death—just
like my mother. The cancer was everywhere in her lungs.

For forty-eight hours I'd watched over her constantly. I
knew when I went off duty, the next medical resident wouldn't
feel that way. The next resident would know this woman was
not his mother. I should stay to the end, I was thinking. It
won't be long now, and by giving her enough pain medicine I
can protect her from the panic of suffocation. But when it was
time to go off duty, I didn't stay. Maybe I was too tired. Maybe
I was afraid it would look too crazy if I refused to go. But we
were so close to that transition, to the line that I never saw my
own mother cross, and this was my chance to make up for all
that neglect. The chance to save her—I wish—but no, it was
only the chance to help her die.

So I went home to spend the evening with my boyfriend. I
had become involved with my classmate David in the fourth

year of medical school, after my marriage dissolved. In his yearbook picture, David is sitting on his motorcycle, wearing goggles, a helmet, and a white doctor's coat. He had grown up in Pennsylvania, where he learned to ski, climb, hike, and ride motorcycles. My idea of adventure was walking through a dangerous neighborhood in New York City. David was my latest passionate and difficult relationship, and in my therapy I talked about little else. I'd made some progress—this time I felt as if I actually liked the man I was with. Yet I still kept my distance, and tonight, while I was physically present with my boyfriend, my heart was with the woman I'd left behind at the hospital, the mother I still wanted to save. She was the one I was loyal to, the one I wanted, the one who filled me with guilt when I thought of leaving her to love someone new.

I was standing alone in my kitchen thinking this was enough. I was a little high from the wine I'd been drinking. Maybe I wouldn't be thinking like this if I were sober. But I'm twenty-seven now, one failed marriage behind me. It's not easy to put a life back together. Is it even worth it? For sixteen years my primary connection had been to someone who no longer existed, and to the utterly irrational hope that I could undo what was done and bring her back to life. What would happen now if I admitted that all my drive and effort to become a doctor would come to naught? Could I even go on? I couldn't, not like this. And what about being close to a man? Could I ever allow myself to be back in the position where abandonment could rip me apart like that again? And what would my lonely life be like if I couldn't? For the first time in my life, the thought crossed my mind: I could jump out the ninth-floor window of this apartment and kill myself. I was amazed that I had never considered this solution before. In the months that followed, the thought would repeatedly occur to me. I did have a choice. I could stop fighting so hard, stop trying to save people who couldn't be saved, stay loyal to my mother and never replace her. I could avoid the risk of devastating loss, quiet every painful thought. But I never made the slightest gesture, never even came close. The force of my mother's struggle to go on living was an indelible example for me. But the loneliness had become intolerable as well, and my loyalty to her weakened. I saw no alternative, so I talked to Mom, heart to heart, aloud. Mom, listen, I can't continue like this, you can't be first anymore. I have to say good-bye to you finally. I'm here with the living, and I need to move on.

The next time I saw my therapist, I did my best to describe how little sense my life made to me. I was trying to save people who couldn't be saved, I told him, but if I gave up trying, I didn't see how I could continue to practice medicine. I claimed I wanted to be close to men, and yet all the while I didn't trust any of them, so why did I keep working at it? And if I couldn't let another person become more important than my dead mother, I'd never have a family of my own. Somehow, just the act of explaining, of finding the words to describe my dilemma, made me feel braver.

I shed a layer of my adolescent numbness, let down my guard, and allowed myself to experience my love for David. Fall came, and we were on vacation in New Hampshire, where the leaves had turned such bright colors it looked as though the trees were brushed with Day-Glo paints. We were in a cabin, logs were burning in the fireplace, and I was feeling an incredible warmth and closeness. But David was depending on my distance to feel safe with me, and now that I had disrupted our previously agreed-upon equilibrium, he began to withdraw. Wanting only what was unavailable, David picked this moment to declare he didn't love me anymore. Now I felt a familiar cold terror, desertion, the permanent end of something I was not at all prepared to relinquish. Having finally taken the risk to love, I was now experiencing only abandonment again.

"I know it's better to be able to love, even if it doesn't work out, but no man will ever love me in return." My therapist was listening, and I didn't know how much more alone I would have felt if I didn't have this place to talk, a place where all the attention was focused on me and I could permit someone to help me find my way. I finished my long, despairing description of how unlovable I was. "But I love you," my therapist announced, a parent reassuring the child he'd helped raise over these past five years. He was married with three children of his own, and I guess he had found room for yet another, a foundling. His words were even more surprising than David's, and they had the profound effect of allowing me to believe a man might love me after all. Being listened to is a form of care one can reasonably expect from a therapist, but being loved seemed something altogether unexpected. Yet of course he remained only my therapist, despite my longing to be his real child, to have a real parent again, to feel whole and no longer envious. Although I was convinced that healing required reclaiming what I had lost, I was quite wrong. I was still years away from understanding what true healing requires: repairing internal wounds, burying the dead, and moving on.

Chapter 10

THE LIFE OF THE MIND

(1973–1975)

I am in a room filled with middle-aged women wearing nothing but short white hospital gowns. They look identical—heavyset, disheveled, blank-faced, and robotic from the effects of the drugs they have been given. I try to talk to them, but they only stare impassively.

I woke up anxious and distraught. The dream reinforced my fear that I had made the wrong decision, and I lay there dreading the first day of my psychiatric training. I'd decided to follow in the footsteps of own therapist, my symbolic father, and become a psychiatrist, even training at the same institution.

But I didn't know whether I'd chosen a new profession or run away from the old one.

I felt unsuited to the practice of medicine. It was confusing to try to save people who wanted to die, and distressing to fail to save people who wanted to live. And with patients in the chronic stages of illness, when living and dying were not at stake, I found myself more strongly drawn to their unique stories than to the repetitive patterns of their diseases. On the last day of my medical training, I was saying good-bye to a woman I'd been treating for hypertension for more than a year. At each visit, I would check her blood pressure, adjust her medication, and make small talk. But on her last visit, she blurted out her entire life story, how she had married a man she didn't love, how she had tried to leave, how her family had threatened to disown her if she did. She was still with him to this day, but even at fifty-eight she thinks if she ever had the courage she would pack up and walk out. She's waited all this time, until the last day she would ever see me, to decide it was safe enough to tell me her story. But now I was embarking on a different career, one in which I would help patients talk at the first meeting instead of waiting for the last. If I couldn't bring my mother back to life, maybe I could fix things by discovering the words for what Mom and I could never express.

It was 9 AM and I was sitting in a room with my new colleagues, the eight men and two women who were starting training with me, all strangers. The chief resident had arrived to orient us. "Look around at the people in this room," he announced. "By the time your training ends, you will be closer to each other than you've ever been to anyone else in your lives." His speech, even with the farcically melodramatic flourishes, made me panic. I wasn't sure I wanted to be close to anyone, let alone to this randomly assembled group of people. I felt like running away, but under the circumstances, that seemed ill advised.

The speech concluded, and we set out on a tour of the psychiatric ward I'd be working on. I was relieved that the patients did not look like those in my nightmare. Some wore ordinary street clothes and behaved in reasonably ordinary ways, but others were in pajamas, pacing or talking incoherently, gesticulating aimlessly. How was I ever going to carry on a conversation with people in such condition? My heart was starting to beat faster. Soon it was pounding. I couldn't breathe. I felt I was about to faint, even die. I stood immobilized, unable to say a word, until the acute fear started to subside and I made it to the nearest telephone.

"Eric, you've got to come right away. I'm completely panicked, and you've got to get me out of here." I had known Eric since he was an intern and I was a third-year medical student. He was five feet ten but weighed only 119 pounds. He claimed that when he was weighed at his army physical, the examiner told him, "Sonny, put your other foot on the scale." Eric was the first friend I'd made—at least the first from whom I didn't feel some sense of detachment—since my elementary school days with my best friends Sarah and Rita. After four hundred sessions of psychotherapy, I could finally do again what had once been so effortless: enjoy the give-and-take of a shared inner life and the mutual certainty of being helped in times of trouble. Eric was in the same psychiatric training program, one year ahead of me. He liked rescuing people in trouble— and now I really needed some rescuing. He came immediately, took me for a long walk, and stayed with me until my panic receded. I was ready to go back to work, and so began my career as a psychiatrist.

I needn't have worried about carrying on a conversation

with my patients: a psychiatric interview doesn't follow the conventions of ordinary conversation. We skip the social niceties and encourage the patient to come right to the point. "I'm the Second Coming of Christ. Notify the media. Go. Call them right away." The thirty-nine-year-old Puerto Rican man was staring at me with a beatific smile. He was very happy, and I started to share his joy, so much so that I was afraid I'd start giggling—not exactly the most professional approach.

But with practice, I became comfortable and matter-of-fact, and learned to ask the questions that form a road map of the mind. I labeled what I saw and heard with scientific terms— delusions, hallucinations, thought disorders—and the phenomena seemed less strange, or frightening, or funny. I learned psychiatry's diagnoses: mania, schizophrenia, borderline personality; and the theories that are put forth to explain the phenomena: the Oedipus complex, the schizophrenogenic mother, the malfunction of neurotransmitters in the brain. Just like in medicine, we started out taking care of the sickest patients, where what's wrong is both urgent and obvious, and where our medical training was still paramount.

Psychiatry is a respite from death but not from suffering. The residents took turns on call in the emergency room. Here I saw a woman who'd had a stroke during the height of sexual excitement and was now afraid to have an orgasm ever again. A man who had been riding the subway for three days without eating or sleeping because imaginary persecutors would catch up with him if he stopped for even a minute. One woman arrived at the emergency room having walked miles to get here. She had no money for car fare, and this was the only hospital she trusted. She had a daughter, she told me, and she loved the little girl, but she had impulses to beat her, just as she was mercilessly beaten herself when she was a child. It was horrible to think of beating a child, but my heart went out to her in her struggle to stay in control. The police brought in a couple who had caused a disturbance by having a violent fight in public. The man wouldn't let his girlfriend talk to me alone, and judging from the gist of their conversation and the flashy clothes they were wearing, I had the distinct impression that she knew secrets about his connections to organized crime. I was standing there envisioning Don Corleone coming after me with a machine gun because I knew too much. Please don't tell me about it! Sometimes I wondered if I was becoming paranoid myself.

One day a patient I was examining actually pulled a knife on me. "Put that knife down, Mr. Jones!" I shouted in the most authoritative tone I could muster, and I was surprised and relieved when he followed my orders. A woman who lived nearby was brought to the emergency room because she had been throwing all her furniture out the window. I was interviewing her in a little room that had a bathroom in the back. I was called away for a phone call, and when I came back she was gone. I could hear water running in the bathroom, and I opened the door. There she was, stark naked, hair thoroughly soaped up, water dripping all over the floor. "I needed a shampoo," she said amicably. Manic, I decided.

I was evaluating a thin, pale young woman, hunched over, timid, speaking barely above a whisper. She started to explain that an evil person was living inside her, and of course I took the description to be a metaphor. I was briefly interrupted, and when I returned I was startled to see a different person sitting in the chair. When I looked more closely, I realized that it was the same person. She sat upright, now wearing bright red lipstick, dark sunglasses, a different hairstyle. She started to shout and spit, cursing the body she claimed she lived inside. I'd read *The Three Faces of Eve*, but I couldn't believe there was a real-life version of the story. The existence of multiple personality disorder is a matter of debate, but I was taken aback by whatever phenomenon I was witnessing. It was an amazing and fascinating place, this emergency room, and I was beginning to think that, yes, maybe I had made the right choice in deciding to become a psychiatrist.

It is remarkable how dismissive many doctors can be of patients who manifest any psychological disturbance. A fifty-year-old woman arrived in the emergency room. She was a bookkeeper by profession, and she had been crying for weeks. She'd been given an antidepressant by her internist, but she hadn't gotten better, and now she'd been getting lost going between work and home. I was worried that her psychological symptoms were part of a neurological disorder, so I referred her to the medical intern. He examined her but reported that he found nothing wrong. "A schizophrenic if I ever saw one," he announced conclusively, although the woman had no symptoms whatsoever of that disease. So I looked in her eyes with my own ophthalmoscope, just to make sure, and there it was: papilledema. Her depression turned out to be the result of a glioblastoma, a malignant brain tumor that is almost always rapidly fatal, even with the best treatment available.

I took the intern aside to privately ask him how he could have written down in her chart that the optic disks were normal. I could see that he was embarrassed, that at least he knew he'd done something profoundly wrong, that he wanted to learn something. But it was discouraging to discover that a doctor's fear of a patient's behavior could be so profound that it drove him away from uncovering even the most elementary objective facts of her case.

Then there were the gifted clinicians, the ones who aston-
ish with their ability to understand another's distress. I was
showing a fourth-year medical student how to interview a psychiatric patient, but I somehow had the impression that she
was already better at it than I was. I felt powerfully drawn to
her special ability to listen and understand, that same powerful empathy I had in childhood with Rita and Sarah, and it
was wonderful to be free enough again to experience it, even
pursue it. We became best friends. So now I had two great
friends, Eric and Franny, just like long ago, and I was becoming part of the world again.

I reconstructed my life without my biological family. I still visited my foster home regularly, celebrating holidays and important events in the lives of my acquired siblings, but my contact with my own brother and sister dwindled away. Henry
had taken off without leaving a forwarding address, and I had
not heard from him in years. Alexis was busy traveling around
the world, though she kept me abreast with letters from the
West Coast, from Europe, from Asia. My grandmother's
dementia had progressed to the point where she no longer rec-
ognized people. Once in a while, I would telephone my aunts
and uncles, who always greeted me with the complaint that I
never called them. Finally, it occurred to me that in fact it was
they who never called me, so I decided to stop pursuing them.
Four years of silence went by, so the call from Uncle Milton
was something of a surprise. "Your grandmother died," he
informed me. "And the funeral is tomorrow." But I had already
grieved for Grandma. It was only her body that was now dead.
This time I was the one who rejected the idea of attending a
funeral with my aunts and uncles. I'd grown willing to

acknowledge that in good times they had no interest, and in bad times they were useless. I declined the invitation, and Milton was outraged. With that, the pretense that I was still a member of my mother's family was no longer possible. At least it was a solution: I was now free of the frustrating fantasy that someday my aunts and uncles would care about me, and I could concede that I would have to find support elsewhere whenever I needed help.

It was convenient to see my therapist at the medical center where we both now worked. One day, ten minutes into my session, he announced that he needed to stop because he was having chest pain. Thirty-nine years old, he'd only been back to work for three weeks since recovering from his first heart attack. He nodded to conclude the session, but I didn't leave. I watched as he called his cardiologist, and yes, the cardiologist said, he should go to the emergency room.

I didn't need a specialist to tell me this. I'd seen plenty of heart attacks, and I'd seen the flat line on the monitor, too. Outcomes vary, but one thing is certain: when death comes, it almost always comes fast, caused by the immediate irritability of heart muscle deprived of oxygen. The regular rhythm of the heart is easily derailed, replaced by no rhythm at all or by an out-of-control beat that is deadly. Time was not in our favor. We were in the private-practice wing of a large hospital, connected to the emergency room by underground tunnels but completely separated from the bustle of doctors and nurses with their crash carts, their medicines, their thoroughly rehearsed procedures. "I'll walk you there." We started out, through the hallway, down the elevator. All the while I was planning my strategy: if he crashes, I'll conduct a cardiopulmonary resuscitation on the floor or in the elevator. I'll enlist the aid of others to do what I can't do alone. I examined passersby, trying to choose the likely ones. I saw myself pounding on his chest, breathing for him, reviving him. I won't screw it up this time. This time I'll know what I didn't know with my own mother. I'll know how to bring him back to life. I dreaded the thought of being put to the test, and I was hoping that I could quickly pass on the responsibility to other doctors who didn't have my personal stake in the outcome.

We completed the trek through the tunnel and caught the elevator going up. Then a short walk and we were in the emergency room. To my relief, my favorite nurse was on duty. "Peggy, this is my psychiatrist, and he's having chest pain and he just got over a previous heart attack and . . ." She didn't say a word. With one hand she grabbed a stretcher, with the other the sleeve of the chief medical resident. In moments, we had a cardiogram going. Should I be looking at this, the inside workings of my therapist's body? I was at first compelled to look, and then terrified by what I saw on the tape reeling out of the EKG: the sure signs of another myocardial infarction. The resident had already found a bed in the coronary care unit, but first I went over to his stretcher to see him off. He lay there naked from the waist up. Incredibly, it occurred to me that he didn't have enough chest hair! How could I be thinking of my preference for hairy chests at a time like this? I leaned over the stretcher and looked into his eyes. He was a little high from the Demerol they'd given him, and he took my hand, staring back at me with appreciation. They wheeled him away.

I stood there, stunned, numb. But from what? From the tragedy of my young therapist's weak heart, the fear that he could die, the memory of the imaginary resuscitations I'd performed as we walked here, or the sight of his hairless chest revealing that he was not, after all, as perfect as I believed? I was in a daze for almost a week. I wondered if I was jinxed, if that's why his heart attack happened at that moment. How many parents could get ill and leave me before it started to look suspicious? Oscar Wilde said that losing one parent is a misfortune, but losing both begins to look like carelessness. What would it look like to lose a third? Fortunately, he survived.

After my therapist's heart attack, I got angry at fatherlike men in general, but of course I left him out of it. After all, I couldn't get angry at someone who was ill, even if he had scared me half to death by getting sick right in front of me, confirming my theory that I was very dangerous, and then deserted me for months of convalescence so I could stew about it all by myself. Instead, I picked one of my supervisors as a target, the tall blond one who was so irritatingly sure of himself. I'd been assigned to present cases to him, to discuss and debate the complex details of psychiatric diagnosis and treatment, but more often than not I was distracted by his hands. He was missing parts of two fingers, and I wondered how he had lost them—I was preoccupied yet again with someone's missing body parts. Once he told me that a woman patient of mine might be having orgasms without knowing it. I took his comment as an insult to all women, and I decided it was time to demolish him: "I don't know about the women you treat," I replied, "but when I have an orgasm, I can tell—there's really no mistaking it." Another time he dropped off his own private patient in the emergency room on his way home at night, staying just long enough to convey his instructions. I disagreed with everything he told me, so I ignored his commands. The next day, we got into a fight over it, each of us enraged at the other. "If you care about your patients so much, why don't you hang around and see things through?" Bull's-eye, I thought, self-satisfied. Therapy was dangerous for me—it had unleashed my angry feelings about being abandoned by men and exposed my struggle: either they didn't measure up, or I didn't.

Since my anger was a complex mixture of the rational and the irrational, expressing it didn't always serve me well. Often I used it constructively, carefully selecting the causes and principles to defend, taking care to get in only the fights I could win. And this anger, whatever else could be said about it, certainly drove me to work hard. Yet just as surely, my conflicting desires to be close to men and to drive them away with my rage created painful struggles in both my professional and personal lives.

Our second year of training was spent on the long-term therapy unit, which was run by a famous psychoanalyst. Most of the patients were young, white, intelligent, of privileged background. But they had very disturbed personalities—borderline, as they are called. "I'm connected to my mother by an invisible umbilical cord," my new patient told me. She was a pretty blond twenty-year-old, and the image she chose had some appeal for me. I had no clear understanding of how adult children ordinarily think about their parents. In college, I watched my roommate Paula interacting with her mother and father as if I were an anthropologist observing Trobriand Islanders, unfamiliar even with their ordinary everyday customs, much less with the complex emotions that underlay their actions. In my apprenticeship as a psychiatrist, I had now learned to label the mature and the infantile, though I was ill

at ease with these terms and unsure where lay the boundary
between science and name-calling. My supervisor listened
attentively as I explained my new patient's childlike complaint. It was here in supervision that I most appreciated my
new profession. I was impressed by how much complexity my
teachers saw in human behavior, and excited by the prospect
of solving the riddle of how another person thinks and feels.
And of course there was no question that my desire to help
another describe and tolerate what is painful was intertwined
with my search to do so for myself.

Most of the patients on the long-term therapy unit broke
my cardinal rule: they lost control. They shouted and
screamed at the slightest provocation, cut their wrists, swallowed too many pills, figured out ways to upset everyone. But
we were prepared for it. We watched them constantly, confronted them at every turn, and discussed their rageful feelings
in group and individual sessions. There was a lot to learn here
about the nature of human desperation. The unit had an
atmosphere of *us* vs. *them*. *Us* was the staff, the ones who knew
better, who had the keys to the locked ward, who huddled in
meetings to discuss what to do with *them*, the unfortunates we
were trying to fix. I felt ill at ease being an *us*, probably
because when I was a foster child I felt very much like a *them*.
The new role didn't suit me, but I tried my best to pass.

Then one day I had to accompany one of my patients to an
interview at the JCCA for placement in a residential program
for emotionally disturbed adolescents. Little did my patient
know that we were taking a trip to my alma mater. We arrived
at the Madison Avenue office, where we stepped into the elevator, and I was horrified to see the nurse I was so fond of, Miss
Coburn, standing there. "Hi, Francine," she said enthusiasti-
cally, and then asked what had brought me back here. I am

accompanying someone to an interview, I answered, and then
stared at Miss Coburn, silently warning her not to blow my
cover. She caught on fast, nodded sagely, and said not one
more word. My patient and her mother seemed content to be
with a doctor who knew her way around this place. I sighed in
relief.

There are many theories in psychiatry, and they often contra-
dict one another. For example, on the long-term unit we tried
to help patients stay away from their families, since it
appeared that growing up in those families was what had
caused their difficulties in the first place. So now we were
going to show them a better way of being. But then I attended a course in family therapy. Here, the teacher believed that
the sick patient was a scapegoat for the entire family's problems, and the only way to get anyone better was to treat them
all together. Shortly after I left the ward, a famous researcher
came and explained that it was all a matter of chemical imbal-
ances in the brain, and that the way to cure it was by giving
medicine. I had the impression that some psychiatrists picked
a theory and stuck to it just because it made things less confusing, and I watched these colleagues lining up on one side or
the other. But I didn't join any camps. I was used to being confused, to being without religion, to not belonging to any one
family, to piecing things together on my own. To me, everything was interesting, but nothing was definitive.

While some theories seemed to me unlikely, I kept my
opinions to myself and worked my way around them. I didn't
believe in the schizophrenogenic mother because I couldn't
really imagine how anything a mother could do would make a
child develop the overwhelming symptoms of schizophre-

nia—see things that aren't there, hear voices, talk incoherently. Besides, I wanted to think children weren't totally at the mercy of what the adults around them do, because if they were, then I'd really have to wonder about my own mental health—and I did enough of that already. I didn't believe in losing control, and it was painful to watch these borderline patients lay bare their innermost conflicts by acting outrageous. My new patient tried to cut his wrist with a butter knife. I took him aside, quietly. "Do you realize how expensive this treatment is, and how long a waiting list we have of people who want to be here?" No, my patient hadn't considered that. "Well, if you want to try to kill yourself instead of trying to get better, you're using up a valuable place that someone else could benefit from." I felt like a heretic, telling my patient to stop joining in with the others and striving to truly express himself. But it had the intended effect: he never tried it again. I was determined that my patients be well behaved. Just like me.

I was not sure I was any better cut out for psychiatry than for internal medicine. My patients fascinated me, but they exhausted me. "You identify too strongly with your patients," my supervisors told me. It was true: I felt a sort of communion with the other, just like with Mom, a feeling of being flooded by her emotions and then deciding that the answer was to join them, be one with them, and so find the way to fix them. So it was that I sat with a helpless patient and felt helpless, or a sad patient and felt close to tears, or a frightened patient and found myself barely able to contain my own panic. Pull yourself together, I'd silently admonish myself, maintain some distance, you can't fix something if you're drowning in it. I was able to conduct at most three of four therapy sessions before feeling completely depleted by the effort.

It was my fourth outpatient visit with a young woman from South America who was suffering from depression. "I'm supposed to leave this weekend for Argentina to participate in a political assassination, but I'm not really feeling up to it. Would you mind writing me a letter explaining my problem?" First, I wondered whether this was some kind of psychotic delusion. But she didn't seem psychotic. In fact, she was perfectly coherent in every other way, and since political assassinations do take place, someone must be committing them. Why not her? And in her present condition, she certainly wasn't up to assassinating anyone. Then I tried to think exactly how a doctor's excuse from an assassination might be worded. The phrase "To Whom It May Concern" had never seemed to me more appropriate, and so I began. "Ms. X is under my care," I continued, "and is not well enough to leave the country." Yes, that sounds neutral enough. I'm not taking any political position or suggesting anything about her ability to load and fire a gun. I'm glad none of my colleagues knows I'm doing this. I completed the letter, signed it, and handed it to her—on hospital stationery, it certainly looked official enough. On the way home, I panicked. What if one of her fellow assassins thinks I know the details of the plot and is lying in wait for me? I could be breathing my last. I arrived at my apartment building. No one there. I opened the door to my apartment and peered in, just in case. No one there either. I thought I must be losing it. It was only 6 PM, but I climbed into bed and fell asleep. This was indisputably an absorbing profession, but I was beginning to think that a little less absorption might be helpful if I was going to pursue it.

Chapter 11

A FAMILY OF MY OWN

(1975–1979)

O f all the things I most wanted but least expected to
have, a family of my own was first. But I had come up
with a solution to my lack of family, the usual answer for me:
work. There was always plenty of that, since people get sick
twenty-four hours a day, seven days a week. And since I was
not sure giving up medicine for psychiatry was the right thing
in the first place, I kept a hand in internal medicine (and
made extra money) by moonlighting in a hectic emergency
room. Here was where I spent most holidays: Thanksgiving,
Christmas, New Year's Eve, the Jewish High Holy Days—I

made sure to volunteer to be on call for all of them, and for any other days that might make me feel lonely or sad.

Morrisania City Hospital ER on New Year's Eve was not a party. I got the medical cases (overdoses, heart attacks), the surgical resident took the trauma (gunshots, car accidents), and there was plenty to go around. The surgeon was busy with a knife wound to the lung. He had the chest sliced open and his hand was inside. The heart had stopped beating on its own, so he was manually pumping it to keep the blood flowing. While one fist was full of this man's heart, the other gripped the telephone. He was consulting with a senior colleague on backup call. My own case was somewhat less dramatic: a sixty-seven-year-old woman with pulmonary edema. Her lungs were full of fluid and she could barely breathe. She reached into her purse and showed me her bottle of digitalis—confirmation, which I hardly needed, that she was in heart failure. "What did you eat tonight, Mrs. Rosen?" I asked, although I was quite sure what kind of answer I was going to get. "Matzo ball soup," she gasped. Bingo! I said to myself. And then, aloud, "Mrs. Rosen, you can't eat matzo ball soup when you have heart failure. It's full of salt. Salt isn't good for you." I proceeded to treat her, knowing full well that this wouldn't be my last case of chicken-soup poisoning for the night.

Mrs. Rosen wasn't the only one having trouble breathing. In our makeshift asthma room—centrally located so we could get there fast—were a half dozen patients, mostly recent immigrants, whose lungs had registered a definitive protest against the quality of our city's air. Each was being treated with injections of epinephrine and intravenous hydration, a procedure that would restore their breath, at least until the next attack. I had just succeeded in resolving a severe attack in a seventeen-year-old girl—she had finally started breathing more or less normally—when her mother burst into the room to continue an argument that had been interrupted when her daughter's asthma first began to act up. Wild gesticulation accompanied rapid-fire Spanish, volume rising. I didn't understand a word of it, but I could see the level of hysteria growing and my patient beginning to gasp for air. Better get this mother out of here before she causes real trouble. The nurse and I had begun to physically shove her out of the room when I saw the daughter turn blue. She had stopped breathing completely. I grabbed an Ambu-bag and started pumping air into her lungs, but it didn't seem to be working. Her brochospasm was so severe that the pressure of the bag wasn't high enough to force air into her. So I took a piece of gauze, placed it over her open mouth, bent back her neck, and started mouth-to-mouth resuscitation—looks great on TV, but it's hardly the normal procedure in a well-equipped modern hospital. But there was no way I was going to let a mother-daughter argument kill one of the warring parties. Not on my shift. My life-guard procedure was effective—I got her breathing again, and she was transferred to one of the medical wards—but my colleagues wouldn't let me hear the end of it. Every time someone was brought in breathless, especially if the patient looked a little disheveled, someone had to yell, "Get Francine—we need mouth-to-mouth on this guy!"

"What's wrong?" I asked my next patient. The fifty-three-year-old slightly unkempt man pointed to his leg. "It hurts." I asked him how long his leg had been hurting. "Twenty years," he said.

"So why did you come to the emergency room at four A.M. on New Year's Eve?" I responded, preoccupied with some of the more bloodily obvious cases around me.

"I couldn't sleep."

I was exasperated, but I didn't get angry because I knew exactly how he felt. Four in the morning, can't sleep, no one to talk to. I liked being here, too, in a crowded bustling ER, surrounded by people, even people I didn't know. I was still lonely, of course, just like this man with his aching leg. But as he and I had both figured out, this was a good place to forget how lonely you were.

"When you get married and live in a tree, send me a coconut COD." There was something immensely reassuring about the rhymes in my sixth-grade autograph book, one of the few possessions I still had from my childhood. *"When you get married and your hubby gets cross, pick up the broom and say you're the boss."* As twelve-year-old girls, we simply expected it to happen: we'd all marry and have babies—everything would fall into place because that is the natural order of things. *"When you get married and have twenty-five, don't call it a family, call it a tribe."* These bits of childhood doggerel found their way into my consciousness and I repeated them to myself. Who knew how difficult it would be to fulfill these seemingly ordinary expectations, and that in fact I might never do so?

Since my relationship with David ended, I'd been living alone, for the first time in my life. No roommates, no husband, no boyfriend. Sometimes I would turn on the TV, the record player, and the radio all at once to obliterate the loneliness of it. Yet I was convinced I needed to do this, to live alone and prove I could be by myself without feeling desperate. My theory—surely not original—was that if I learned to survive without a man, I wouldn't feel so eager to throw myself into something that had little chance of success. I became more lighthearted, dated men I found fun, and envisioned a life for myself as a single woman.

"Yes, I read *Fear of Flying*. It's OK, if you don't know any better," said the voice at the other end of the telephone. I was making small talk with someone I'd never met. One of the psychiatric residents I was training with had asked me if I'd like to meet his old college roommate, someone a little different from all the doctors we were surrounded by, someone who was completing a Ph.D. in French literature and had recently broken up with his girlfriend. Despite my belief that I could manage alone, I really didn't want to, and I was always willing to meet someone new. Erica Jong's novel about her sexual exploits was all the rage at the moment—I felt sorry for the poor psychiatrist the author used to be married to. I would never reveal the details of my personal life in a book!

"Excuse me, but my doorbell just rang. It's the police—I'll call you back." Nick had to pick this moment to call: was he really going to believe that some strange man had been throwing pebbles at my window all evening and that I'd had to call the cops to get rid of him? Or would he just assume he'd called a nutcase psychiatrist who had allowed her paranoid fantasies to get the better of her?

The police having done their duty, I called back. "What do you look like?" he asked. I described myself: green eyes, brown hair, five feet two, more or less regular.

"And you?"

"Brown. Brown hair, brown eyes, brown mustache. Five feet seven. More or less average." An hour more of conversation, and we arranged to meet.

He appeared at my apartment door, plaid turquoise scarf, dark blue wool cap and coat, smiling. Shiny white teeth. It was nine o'clock on a Monday night in November, and Nick had just finished teaching a French class at Lehman College, not far away. I knew about a dozen words of French. I asked him about the dissertation he was working on at Columbia, and then wondered who this Diderot guy was. We talked on, but soon it was closing time at the Chinese restaurant and a man in a white apron began running a vacuum cleaner around our table, clearly suggesting that the last of the lingerers should now leave. Nick took me home without saying he'd call, and I really couldn't tell if he would. I had a good time, but did he like me or not? When I picked up the phone two days later and heard his voice, I was thrilled, but weeks later, once I realized that he really cared for me, after the lyrical French poetry and the candlelight dinners, after I discovered that I was with a regular man, the kind who still believed that a breakfast of scrambled eggs and English muffins with cream cheese was health food, after I understood that he was undamaged and actually available, I panicked.

He must be crazy to fall for me just like that! Nick enjoyed my absorption in my career, teased me about the ridiculous hours I worked, found my Bronx accent amusing, had barely a critical word to say. Where was the familiar struggle to win him over, the pain and suffering when it didn't work, the realization that if I was hoping for a family of my own, I'd made yet another mistake? I was not expecting a man who really wanted me—I was so accustomed to selecting unavailable men that the warm welcome actually scared me. "Don't worry," he said. "I really like you, but if it doesn't work for you, I can leave." I calmed down. There was an escape. Not like when I had to reject the idea of heaven because I couldn't tolerate the prospect of being trapped, even in a good place.

Nick was funny and sociable, so he got along with all my friends, and we spent our time relaxed, laughing, having fun. He was also modest and direct, with a slightly depressive view of life that made me feel right at home. I was listing the daily events that made me feel guilty. "You're guilty you're alive," Nick summarized. At last, a man who understands me! He had never been inside a therapist's office—why would anyone want to tell a complete stranger his personal business? He kept his own counsel, like Mom, and he was passionate about what was right and wrong, which I was sure was how Dad must have been. Very quickly, he seemed like family. It was difficult to have a fight with him—I would say it's my fault, he would say no, it was his fault, and we would continue to compete for the blame until the argument came to a sputtering halt. Nick loved books, words, and language. He sized people up quickly, and he was not very likely to change his mind. He sized me up, too. After two weeks, he concluded he wanted to marry me. Fortunately, he waited three months to inform me. Now I began to experience my relationship with Nick as something comfortable and familiar, the way it was with Mom when looks and touch and gesture were more powerful than words, and you know you're really home.

Considering my scientific inclinations, I have a very superstitious streak. To avoid disaster, for example, I think it's important to do the opposite of whatever happened before the last catastrophe. So when I married Nick, exactly a year and a day after meeting him, I repeated nothing from my first marriage—no engagement, no white gown, no big party afterward. Instead, I bought a short cotton dress with brown and yellow and orange leaves, a perfect representation of the late

November day of our wedding. We'd found a justice of the peace, and Nick's two brothers came along as witnesses.

It wasn't much of a family affair. Alexis was now wandering through India, and it had been eight years since I had last heard from Henry. As the middle child, the one who stayed put and could therefore always be found, I was in the best position to serve as our center, but the center did not hold. All siblings treat one another badly from time to time, or harbor feelings of anger and guilt. But it seemed in our case, because terrible things had in fact occurred, that our feelings had come true, that we had actually harmed one another and had each been punished: my brother tormented us and was twice banished; I was sent away when I expressed a wish to abandon my sister and live with Aunt Milly; and Alexis, after I left our foster home, developed a conflicted relationship with Erma based on finally conceding that I had maliciously come between them. The fear that we would undermine one another made avoidance seem the best solution. To reestablish ourselves, we went our separate ways. But Nick loved his two brothers, considered them his closest friends. Their presence would suffice.

Nick was driving. It was slow motion. I felt excited, scared, and unreal all at once. How did I find this man? Was this an arranged marriage worked out by a colleague who had more sense of what I needed than I could ever know? Had I come back to life enough to choose a man who loved me? Was I on my way to a wedding or a funeral, and how could I explain the fusion of joy and terror? We arrived at the judge's private house in Irvington, New York, and ten minutes later we'd said our "I do"s and we were married. I was wondering if it really took, unsure whether a ceremony so unceremonious could still count. Then Nick's younger brother insisted on taking a picture of us in front of our 1969 Chevrolet, since, he claimed, when it comes to pictures of weddings, it's not the participants that interest people—it's looking at all those antique cars. For a honeymoon, we headed to Washington Irving's Sunnyside estate nearby and spent three hours walking through the grounds. In the gift shop, I bought a picture of the Headless Horseman. A terrified boy on a horse is being pursued by a monstrous headless man. Maybe that was me on my wedding day: a woman who was still not certain if she could be or should be part man, who survived when she should have died, who was trying to quietly steal some happiness when she should instead have stayed loyal to her dead parents, and who was unsure what the punishment would be for this transgression. When we arrived back home, Henry called to say that he had settled down in Cleveland, Ohio—and I couldn't fathom how he happened to select this particular day to suddenly reappear. That night, Nick's parents and my foster family came for dinner. The next week, I framed the picture of the Headless Horseman in wedding white and hung it in the bathroom, the place where I had once explained to Alexis all about Mom's death. It still hangs there today.

As a wedding present, Nick's parents gave us two tickets to visit them in Tokyo, where Nick's father was stationed for a work assignment. Fifteen hours' flight time from New York, with a stop in Seattle, thirteen hours on the return trip—and I was terrified of flying. I was unsure how anyone could be comfortable turning control of her life over to strangers, and I was convinced that the laws of physics made no sense if they allowed something as heavy as a jet airplane to hang in midair. But our trip to Japan was magical, and our return trip uneventful, until four hours into the flight.

A flight attendant was striding down the aisle, somber and purposeful, his eyes fixed firmly on me. My first thought was that the plane was having mechanical trouble, yes, that's it— but why would he pick me among all these passengers as the first one to inform? He squatted next to my seat and quietly said that the passenger roster listed me as a doctor, and could I come and take a look at a passenger who appeared to be ill. He led me forward and stopped at the seat nearest the bulk-head. A woman was in the midst of a severe asthma attack— I'd seen hundreds of them, and diagnosis was easy. I had no medical equipment, not even a stethoscope, so I pulled up her blouse and put my ear against her back. She was in such severe bronchospasm that I heard no breath sounds at all. She gasped that she had already tried two aminophylline suppositories but they were not working. She had several vials of injectable steroids in her purse—a sure sign that her prior attacks had been severe—but she had no syringes and there were none on the plane. She had brought a positive-pressure respirator with her for use in case her breathing became labored, and was dis-mayed to learn that it was incompatible with the plane's elec-trical system. I was hoping that her panic at this realization was a factor in her attack, because there was no help available here except the psychological. Below us was nothing but the expanse of the Pacific Ocean, and I was terrified that the woman was going to stop breathing altogether. None of this distracted me from my flying phobia—on the contrary, it con-firmed my feeling that we were all going to die.

Still, I took charge. I instructed her to drink cups of water to help loosen the secretions, I monitored her pulse, I repeat-edly listened to her lungs, my ear against her back. I had her use one more suppository, although I was skeptical that another would work where the first two had failed. She wouldn't dare stop breathing on me, I thought, fearfully contemplating what it would be like to handle a respiratory arrest without the equipment and personnel of an ER. She wouldn't dare leave me with yet another death on my conscience.

There was nothing left to do except talk her down. So I kept telling her that her asthma was improving, although I found no evidence that it actually was. The flight attendant told me that in one hour the pilot could make a choice: land in Anchorage, which would take one hour more, or head on to our scheduled stop in Seattle, an additional two hours away. I stared at him, amazed. This entire 747, with all of its three hundred passengers and crew, would land in Anchorage if I gave the word. The flight attendant asked me if there was anything he could do for me. I wanted him to promise me that the plane wasn't going to crash, but knowing such an idiotic request would undoubtedly make him lose all confidence in my medical prowess, I politely declined the offer.

After about forty-five minutes, my largely psychological approach seemed to work: the woman's attack broke, her breathing began to sound normal, and I concluded that we could push on to Seattle. I was relieved both that my patient had recovered and that I wouldn't have to undergo an additional landing and takeoff on this already nerve-racking flight.

I stayed with my patient, now calm and breathing almost normally, but depleted of emotional and physical energy. We sat side by side, in silence. I knew nothing about her, not even her name, but she clearly had no inclination to speak. As the minutes passed, I grew ever more convinced that she wasn't talking because she didn't want me near her one more minute, couldn't stand my presence now that she was breathing comfortably on her own. Finally, sitting there became intolerable, so I told her that I'd return to my seat now, and that if she needed me, I'd come back. Ten minutes later, the flight attendant came back for me, and I spent the rest of the flight quietly seated next to her, observing her rhythmic breathing. It occurred to me that if I didn't feel wanted by someone who believed her life depended on me, then there was no way I could feel wanted by anyone else. But what I couldn't see was how my fury at her for threatening to die on me created the distance that so often served as my protection.

Marrying Nick made me part of a family again. His parents were childhood sweethearts, still in love forty years later. Along with Nick's brothers, they took me in, doted on me, a new beloved daughter and sister, and included me in everything as if I had belonged there all along. In my dreams, though, it was different. Nick didn't love me anymore. Maybe he had found someone else. Maybe he was just tired of me. Maybe he could see beneath my carefully patched-together surface and had discovered the hidden damages. Maybe there was no reason at all, just that nothing lasts and our time was up. "Nick, I had a horrible dream that you didn't love me anymore," and I'd curl up against him and he'd tell me it wasn't true, that it would never be true, and I didn't understand how anyone could feel so certain. My fear would recede, only to return with the next dream.

Nick seemed more interested in my father's family than I was, or at least more systematic in his determination to find whatever traces of them still existed. From an out-of-print books catalog he bought my Uncle John's autobiography, published in the 1930s. Did you know your grandfather was a ne'er-do-well inventor, always dreaming up some new gadget he hoped would make him rich? That your Uncle John was an acquaintance of Chesterton, Yeats, John Masefield? Wait! It gets better! He was Dorothy Sayers's lover! Yes, I guess that's interesting, I told Nick, but I didn't want to read about it. I felt excluded, a stranger.

Undaunted by my lack of enthusiasm, Nick proceeded to track down my father's story. He started where I had left off more than a decade ago, with the microfilms at the Forty-second Street library, found the accounts of my father's trial in 1918, learned that the judge was Kenesaw Mountain Landis (the same vindictive Red-baiting Chicago judge who would later become the first commissioner of baseball), and came home with copies of the newspaper articles. There was my father's name, Alexander Cournos, listed along with more than one hundred other labor organizers convicted in the mass trial. Then Nick had an idea: let's write to Leavenworth—the address on the letter my father had sent his mother—and ask them if they have a photograph of him. I had no picture of my father, and I didn't remember what he looked like. The idea of seeing an actual photograph of him was thrilling, but it seemed a very long shot to me, and I didn't want to get my hopes up in case it didn't work. Incredibly, there was a response, and enclosed was a Xerox copy of a photograph. There was a recognizable man there, and I was astonished. But Nick said we could do better—let's go for the actual photograph. He proceeded to write the director of the prison yet another letter, this time asking to borrow the original photograph and promising to return it after we copied it. This seemed to me extremely unlikely to produce results.

But it worked! My husband found my father! Two weeks later, the actual photograph arrived in the mail; we made a copy and returned the original with a box of chocolates and a note of gratitude. The only photograph of my father shows him with a day's beard, tie loosely knotted beneath a rumpled collar. I imagine that it was taken the day he was arrested. He has dark eyes, dark hair parted on the left and combed back. He gazes straight ahead, very slightly smiling. He is dark and handsome, and, most amazing, he bears a startling resemblance to Nick, a resemblance that everyone who sees the picture remarks upon. Maybe I did somehow remember him. Using an image buried deeply within me, I found a man who looked just like him.

One summer, on vacation with our friends Franny and Eric, sharing a house in the Berkshires, Nick announced, "Have you noticed that Francine does the get-to's?"

"The what?"

"The get-to's. 'I get to do this, you get to do that, he gets to do the other.' " Nick started chuckling at my propensity for sweetly assigning tasks to everyone, dividing them up to make sure we received from each precisely according to his ability and gave to each precisely according to his needs. In fact, deciding who got to do what seemed to be my true calling— more than medicine, even more than treating psychiatric patients, what I felt most at home with was being the boss. It reminded me of childhood, of trying to repair things between Mom and Henry, of monitoring what went wrong so I could step in and fix it, of caring for Alexis and negotiating for Grandma, of deciding that the best thing to do was to take charge.

206 CITY OF ONE

As I neared the end of my psychiatric training in 1976, I cam-
paigned for the job as director of the most chaotic inpatient
unit in the hospital, the community service, the one that
cared for the sickest and poorest patients. This was unquestionably the job with the lowest status in the department of
psychiatry—research, teaching, and taking care of wealthy
people are, in that order, the prestige assignments at an academic medical center. But I'd never been so sure of any career
decision as I was of this one, and I got the job.

Nothing worked right on this service. Nurses quit every few
weeks. Therapy aides got drunk at lunch. Other services in the
hospital sent us patients for no reason except that no one else
wanted them. There weren't enough beds for all the patients
we were supposed to be treating. The psychiatric residents
hated their rotation here. And I felt right at home. No sooner did I solve one problem than another arose.

One day they wheeled onto the ward an unconscious man,
lying on a stretcher and clad in a white hospital gown. "Why
are you bringing an unconscious person onto a psychiatric
ward?" I asked, suppressing my fury.

"We think he's faking it" was the inane reply. I sent the
patient back to the emergency room, where he could receive
the urgent medical attention anyone could see he needed.
Apparently, no one had ever said no to such practices, and my
senior colleagues wanted to know what gave me the nerve to
object. But it wasn't nerve, it was outrage. I was outraged that
this was the kind of treatment my medical center thought
poor people deserved. Fine, I decided, but this is one poor people's medical service that isn't going to work that way. I began
to organize systems and rules to make things sensible and

orderly in a world where the naked emotions of very ill psychiatric patients had to be faced, and faced rationally. I created a boundary around our unit so that we were no longer drowning in the angry demands of colleagues who thought a place with as little status as ours had no right to say no. I found good use for my high tolerance for chaos, and ample opportunity to demonstrate my determination to bring it under control. If life's challenge is to find one's truest self among all the possible selves, I think I met it. I made the community service my permanent place of business, determined to have it deliver better care to patients who had nowhere else to go. I developed a program in the image of my childhood fantasy, one that provides respectful care to people who have no choice, because that's the way all people should be treated, because that's what Dr. Goldstein showed me when I was a child in foster care, because I know how much it means to be treated with dignity when you are powerless. The struggle was exhilarating and frustrating in equal measure, but slowly I gained the upper hand.

It also pleased me that I had married a man who wanted children. I desperately wanted a baby, and during the months I tried without success, I thought of every reason why it couldn't possibly work, how I could never reclaim the parent-child relationship ruptured by death long ago, how my body must be too damaged or too masculine to be suited to this undertaking, how such ordinary happiness was bound to elude me. But then it happened anyway! I was thrilled to be pregnant, but that didn't settle it. I am a doctor, and I know what can go wrong—I'd seen it for myself. I pulled out my obstetrics textbook. For the first trimester, I followed the chart of miscarriage rates.

Midway along, I worried that the baby could die inside me. When I reached term, I imagined the uterus that ruptures in labor, the patient who hemorrhages to death, the baby who strangles on the cord that once nourished him. I'd already fallen in love with this baby that moved and kicked and hiccuped inside me, and the thought of all that loss haunted me.

When I went into labor, the pain frightened me, and I realized more vividly than I had in years that my mother wasn't there, that she could not comfort me or give me advice, ever, and that she'd never meet her grandchild. As the finality of that loss reasserted itself, I cried, and then the pain distracted me. Nick and I left home for the hospital, but during the car ride there a frightening memory intruded, an incident an obstetrician friend once described. Routine term pregnancy, husband in the delivery room. Suddenly the patient's blood pressure drops precipitously. It is a rare complication of pregnancy: a ruptured liver. There is no saving her. She bleeds to death, and the baby dies, too. The despairing husband faces the loss of everything. Suppose that man were Nick. I wish I could fantasize the commonplace, but instead fear of the catastrophic relentlessly turned ordinary expectable outcomes into miracles. It would surely be a miracle if we all lived and the baby was born healthy.

"It's a little lady!" I listened, and she cried: her first breath! I couldn't believe I'd had a girl. A perfect, healthy beautiful one at that. We didn't even have a girl's name picked out. Nick and I had both wanted a girl—each for our own reasons. But we had prepared ourselves for the boy we knew we would love anyway. Five minutes after she was born, the pediatrician handed me my baby girl wrapped in a soft blanket. "She's perfect," the doctor announced. "And see those faint red splotch-es on her eyelids? Those are birthmarks. Ninety percent chance they'll go away in a few months." I stared at the unique patterns on my daughter's eyelids, and memorized them so they couldn't send me home with the wrong baby.

"They'll turn green, just like yours," my mother-in-law announced as she stared into Elizabeth's blue eyes. I was skep-tical, but within a year her prediction came true: Elizabeth's eyes are identical to mine. I liked the ways she resembled me, but I wasn't so sure it was safe for either one of us.

Having Elizabeth was the most ecstatic moment of my life, and the most treacherous, provoking every wonderful and ter-rible emotion I ever felt toward my own mother. It was love at first sight, joy and amazement, great happiness, but the dark side did not disappear. The terror of separation still lurked, threatening to rob me yet again. Maybe it was me who would die now— that's what happens when you become the mother, you get sick and die. Or the other way around: to me, every one of Elizabeth's childhood illnesses was the herald of the angel of death. I lived in fear.

Elizabeth and I built a relationship filled with words. Maybe by her nature she could never have been the kind of child I was, self-contained and unrevealing. Maybe I encour-aged her uncensored self-expression. Maybe she had her father's gift for language, and that's why she so often sat alone on the couch practicing new words aloud. Whatever the explanation, I was fascinated by her developing ability to communicate, and I faithfully recorded her emerging vocal-izations in the baby journal I kept since the day she was born. By the time she was eighteen months old, there were too many words on the list: "Will stop recording vocabulary," the entry reads. Elizabeth noticed every nuance of emotion and offered her observations in a running commentary. My journal records her words at twenty months: "Made Mommy angry. I'm sorry." When she was twenty-three months old, I documented her empathy with another child: "A girl is crying," the journal entry quotes her as saying. "What happened to her? She fell. She cried. I want to cry, too." I was determined to nurture in my child a freedom to communicate I had never enjoyed myself, and I did my best to suppress any expression of my own irrational fears. But as I resonated with Elizabeth's normal developmental anxieties about separation, the feelings began to overwhelm me until finally I could contain myself no longer. I wanted to cry, too.

Chapter 12

CITY OF WOE

(1979–1983)

"O dark dark dark. They all go into the dark, / The
vacant interstellar spaces. . . ." I was reading T. S.
Eliot's *Four Quartets*. Maybe that was where I was, in the
vacant interstellar spaces. Certainly I was nowhere I'd ever
been before, nowhere familiar.

Noises sounded too loud, time went by too slowly, I was
dizzy and weak, as if I'd just come down with a terrible flu. The
smallest exertion seemed too much, but sitting still seemed
just as hard. At a meeting at work, I was so restless I could
have crawled out of my skin. On the clock, it lasted one hour.

In my mind, it lasted five. I was on my way to the dentist, but I wondered if I could make it there and back. It seemed so easy before. How did I do it? I'd left the subway and was starting out on the three-block walk to the office. It could be three miles. Tears were streaming down my face. I was crying for every reason and for no reason at all.

It was as if my skin had peeled away. I felt everything around me. I watched a father carry his sick child from the hospital. I cried as I imagined this complete stranger's pain. I was sitting on the subway reading a sad story in the newspaper, quietly weeping. Maybe people around me thought something tragic had just happened to me. Why else would a young woman be making a public display of her tears? Who could have guessed that it had occurred more than twenty years ago, and that I'd picked this moment to fall apart?

My state of mind was totally altered. I was convinced that no real-life event could inspire this much terror and despair. I used to know how to become numb. Now I was as terrified as if I were living in one of my dreams about being chased by a man with a knife. But this was not a dream. My fear pursued me all my waking hours, unrelenting. At thirty-four, I had been a psychiatrist for six years, but I had never felt I was on this side of madness.

I went through my checklist, assessing my state of mind as I would a patient. I was not psychotic, I reassured myself, no delusions or hallucinations, but I had almost every symptom of major depression, including many attributed to its most severe form.

How did I used to fall asleep? I thought as I lay in bed at 2 A.M., trying to remember the steps involved in something that was once so automatic. But no amount of conscious effort or bodily fatigue could help me, so I went into the living room, lay on the couch, wrapped myself in a sheet, and pretended I was in a shroud in a coffin. Either I was like Mom, and I really was dying, or I was undergoing some dramatic transformation and I'd be reborn. I was frightened by my odd ideas, but it was as if a floodgate between my unconscious and my conscious mind had been opened and all the underlying conflicts and feelings that had been so hard to gain access to in my first analysis were now released.

I was drowning. I was in a raging river and I was clinging to a branch to prevent myself from disappearing over the waterfall. I was grasping a tree on a tiny island with all my might, my legs dangling in the water while the current tried to rip me away. I was trying to reach shore.

I'd joined a pool, exercising regularly for the first time in my life. Paradoxically, swimming was one of the few activities that brought some small relief from my symptoms. I was comforted by the exertion, the sensation of being surrounded by tepid, still water, the reassurance that I could make it to shore with each lap. Sometimes I played a mental game with the person swimming in the next lane. If I didn't reach the wall first on the next lap, I'd die. Swim faster—the Headless Horseman is gaining on you. Your life is at stake. All those feelings I'd kept in such neat compartments in my mind had escaped, merging into a fearsome flood.

Nothing broke my mood. There were no distractions. Music had no sound, food no taste. Was the sun shining or was it raining? No matter: it rained inside me every day. I was driving my car. I thought about how easy it would be to make one wrong turn into a tree and end the suffering. I was walking down the street with my daughter in the stroller. I was my mother. I was about to die and abandon my child. I had an aneurysm in my brain. It would burst and I would die right here this minute. So maybe if I bleed into my brain, I'm really my father. I thought I was becoming demented. My brain was clouded, and I made absent minded mistakes. I put the cereal in the refrigerator, and the milk in the cabinet. I poured the gravy down the sink, while preserving the waste liquid from the vegetables I'd just cooked. I felt so physically ill and fatigued that I thought I must be dying.

By now I had seen a lot of death, but still the hardest was watching my mother die. Slowly, relentlessly, she slipped away from me when I would have done anything—given her half the remaining years of my own life if that were possible—to keep her. As a doctor, I thought I now finally understood where the line between life and death was, and how someone crossed it. But my episode of depression brought all the old fears back, and convinced me that I had both my father's brain tumor—why else is my mind so altered?—and my mother's cancer, which was spreading through my body, just like the terrifying cases I'd seen of people who came to the hospital riddled with metastatic cancer yet were still unaware of it.

I know exactly when my illness began: on June 24, 1979, I woke up next to Nick in our apartment feeling physically sick, tired and nauseated. I was trying to get pregnant with a second child, and I thought maybe I'd succeeded and these were the first signs. But my period came, and the sickness did not go away.

In July, I left for vacation on Cape Cod with Nick and Elizabeth, convinced I had the flu. Elizabeth was twenty months old now, at the height of a phase of separation anxiety, and the change of scenery had only made it worse. I was going out shopping and she started to scream in panic as I walked out the door. A startling thought occurred to me for the first time: Where was my own panic when I lost my mother? I was gripped with anxiety, but I still didn't get it. I still had not concluded that what I felt in my body was being caused by my mind. Three weeks passed, and we returned to the city. Elizabeth had moved on to another stage of development, but I was still trying to work out the separation problem. Now the feeling of depression started to descend. I cried and was unable to sleep. August passed, then Labor Day.

I went to my internist, convinced I was dying, but he found me perfectly healthy. Time passed so slowly. Suppose I never get better? I will suffer this way for an eternity. Nick and my friends had been consistently kind and helpful, but I could tell that they were becoming alarmed. It was clear I had to do something, so I called my former therapist. "Stress," I told him. I'm just stressed out, I think, like any woman trying to raise a baby and pursue a career. As if this could explain my completely altered state of mind. The theory had no staying power.

It had been three years since my last appointment. He had stopped smoking, given up fatty foods, even had bypass surgery. His heart was fine, he let me know, and fit me into his schedule right away, as I trusted he would. Now I had people I could really depend on if I was in trouble. He was one of them. He likes infants—still spends most of his time studying them. So maybe he was prepared for my panic over losing my mother, a feeling of terror much more intense now than when I actually lost her.

I don't think of myself as an easy patient. Although from the start I showed up regularly, paid my bills, was well behaved, and took an instant liking to my therapist, I was terrified by my inner life, which of course was to be the focus of our conversation. The subject of my mother was the most fearful of all. My resistance could be summarized as follows:

"You're angry with your mother."

"No I'm not."

"You idealize her."

"No I don't."

"You're angry at me, too."

"No I'm not. And you're perfect. Just like her."

After all, as long as you're going to have an imaginary mother, why not make her a perfect mother and have your perfect feelings for her? If I no longer had to concern myself with having a real live mother, if I had to invent one, why would I invent a flawed one?

Another advantage to my delusion: when I became a mother myself, I would know just what to do, because I would be just like my own mother. It never crossed my mind that emulating my mother would mean feeling convinced that I was ill and dying, about to desert the child I so desperately wanted to raise.

One day, during a moment of total panic, I did something very uncharacteristic: I called my therapist between sessions. "I think I'm falling apart." He heard my fear, and his response surprised me. "You are falling apart," he said, "but that's because it's safe to fall apart. Now you have the support that permits it." I took his words to mean that this frightening experience nevertheless had some value, could be managed. I found this immensely reassuring. It was true. I had reestablished my life—a husband I loved, an adorable daughter, wonderful friends and colleagues. I was no longer in a struggle for survival where any weakness could be fatal. I could fall apart and put things back together in a new way. I was grateful that psychoanalysts believed in such things. Someone else might have thought I was just losing my mind. And I understood that not falling apart could also be very costly, although this was easier to observe in others than in myself.

I was interviewing a candidate for a job as a physician at my hospital. He was an orphan, too—his father had died when he was ten, and his mother committed suicide two years later. The thought of a mother who leaves on purpose horrified me. He continued his story, but I was now distracted by his manner. His face was devoid of emotion, his speech and movements robotic. His frozen state seemed even more frightening than his mother's act of abandonment. What pain would he have to go through before he could wake up and live again?

"You were right all along," I told my therapist at the next session. "My mother wasn't really ideal."

"Something really is going on with you!" he said. Should it have taken years of therapy to conclude that my mother was not perfect, something so obvious that anyone with a mother would have figured it out years before without seeing a psychiatrist? But figuring it out was not the issue. Twenty years of dammed-up fear, fury, and disappointment were crashing down on me. The thoughts were sickening, literally. Vomit out the past, I was thinking, leaning over the toilet in a bathroom stall at work. Purge yourself. Then you can start over.

Some part of me thought: You can take an antidepressant; it

might make you better. But profound objections came to mind. Denial. I'm not depressed. This can't be happening to me. Shame. I object to labeling myself with an unpleasant disease. Fear. I've lost control and I'm going to regain it all by myself, thank you. Worry. I could try a medicine only to discover it doesn't work and then lose all hope of getting better. And worst of all, taking a medication would prove what I've feared most all along—I'm damaged and defective. If I pretend I'm fine, then this episode doesn't count against me. "Physician, heal thyself"—yes, but the old saying doesn't account for how resistant we can be as patients.

Every day, I dragged myself to work. Fortunately, my program was running smoothly now, and my administrator could fill in for me when some task seemed intolerable. My small private practice consisted of only a few patients I'd been treating for years. I would not even consider taking on anyone new. I maintained a facade of normality that surprised even me.

The chairman of my department urged me to apply to be director of a large department of psychiatry at a hectic city hospital. Between meetings with various staff at the unfamiliar medical center, I felt like an impostor pretending to be a psychiatrist, all the while imagining myself in disturbing or incongruous situations: applying for a position as a child prostitute in a massage parlor, being placed in foster care, jumping out of the hospital's sixteenth-story window. During the interviews, I managed to rally the 10 percent of my brain that still functioned properly to discuss the reorganization of a complex and troubled hospital service. There were two hundred applicants for the job. When they offered it to me, I realized that I was in no condition to take it on: I turned them down. I probably should not have taken pride in my ability to hide my weaknesses so well, but I did. See, Mom? I can do it, too. I learned your methods perfectly. Aren't you proud of me?

It was amazing how much effort it took to pretend I was fine, to talk normally, smile pleasantly, swallow food when I wasn't hungry, sit still when my mind was telling me to bolt and run. The thought of dying seemed frightening, but wouldn't it also be a relief? But despite my suffering, I never even got close to endangering myself. I finally concluded: If I never get better, I will live the rest of my days just like this. I will never kill myself. It's not permitted. My measly depression is nothing compared with my mother's physical torment, her decision to accept every horrible treatment just to spend a little more time with her children. She went to work with end-stage metastatic breast cancer until the day of her final hospitalization when she could no longer breathe, not even a little. She set the standard I strove for, yet in the end she still abandoned me. I must pass on a different legacy.

Despite my self-control, my therapy, and my rage at my symptoms, I could not find a way back to my usual state of mind, and gradually I stopped fighting and learned to wait. I began to think of my episode as a journey, and discovered there was a spiritual aspect to living in those vacant interstellar spaces. My suffering was punctuated by moments of ecstasy, in which I felt at one with the universe. I was sitting on the lawn with Elizabeth on my lap. It was a winter evening, snowing gently. We both looked up at the falling flakes in mutual delight. I had a daughter now. I was part of the world, united with it. I understood now. If I wanted to raise my daughter with the full range of feelings that are possible in such an intense relationship, I would let myself experience the panic and fury I had kept at bay all these years. Maybe then I would be free.

Amazingly, I could still concentrate to read. My refuge, built in childhood, was still there, so I crawled in and searched for the meaning of this terrible experience. I felt desperate to learn from others who had preceded me, to feel less alone. In 1979, subjective descriptions of depression were rare in scientific writing, and what few there were usually reduced feelings to symptoms, defenses, and treatments.

But literature was different. Reading helped me make sense of my strange feelings of spirituality. Phrases from literature became my prayers, and I imbued each with an idiosyncratic meaning. From T. S. Eliot: "I said to my soul, be still, and wait without hope / For hope would be hope for the wrong thing." Meaning: I hope for my suffering to end, but that may be the wrong hope. First I have to complete this journey. From *Hamlet:* "But you must know your father lost a father, / That father lost, lost his. . . ." Meaning: Everyone must face the deaths of their parents—you must accept this universal truth and move on.

I read books about religion and philosophy that did not require belief in the supernatural. Phrases caught my attention and I held on to them: "Abandon the search for God. You will find Him in yourself." "Avoidance of suffering leads to worse suffering," which was why I must face the pain now if I hoped to move past it. I read William James's description of religious melancholy: "The process is one of redemption, not of mere reversion to natural health, and the sufferer, when saved, is saved by what seems to him a second birth, a deeper kind of conscious being than he could enjoy before." Or Herbert Fingarette, who made a link between the religious quest and the psychoanalytic journey: "It is a crisis of suffering and of the movement either toward a saving rebirth of a new self or a self-destroying evasion of the task." All this helped me to

make some sense of my otherwise inescapable pain, to find
some justification for having to grapple with it, to believe that
I could find a new self.

Religious preoccupations are common when the mind is
severely stressed. During my first year of psychiatric training,
I treated a brilliant young man with severe schizophrenia who
saw and heard angels. The angels perfumed his room with
heavenly smells and sent hairs through the air which landed
between the pages of the Bible he constantly carried, serving
as bookmarks that would tell him which passages to read next.
Delusions and hallucinations, I concluded, the diagnosis creating enough distance between us that I felt protected from
his madness. But he rejected my doctorly formulation, insisted on the reality of his angels, and refused the medication I
considered vital to his well-being. I grew attached to this man
and became increasingly familiar with his psychotic world,
easily following his reasoning. And every so often I got scared:
If I could understand him, maybe this was a world I could get
stuck in, too.

I spent more time with Dante and Virgil than with any other
authors. I passed through the circles of hell, then did my time
on the ledges of purgatory. In Ciardi's verse translation of the
Inferno, I came across the best short description of depression
that I've ever read:

> *I did not die, and yet I lost life's breath.*
> *Imagine for yourself what I became,*
> *Deprived at once of both my life and death.*

A perfect description of my own state of mind: neither alive nor dead. In the *Purgatorio*, I saw myself committing each of the seven deadly sins, but the scene that haunted me was the second ledge with the souls who have had their eyes sewn shut to atone for their envy. This was not envy of material possessions, which interested me little. It was a lifetime of envy: as a child, of friends with parents; as an adolescent, of people with handsome chins; as an adult, of those who seemed to achieve so easily the state of contentment that eluded me.

I was convinced that I must repent for my sins. Sometimes, when I was alone in my office, I dropped to my knees and prayed for forgiveness. From whom? I thought I didn't believe in God, but I nevertheless felt compelled to think about my spiritual shortcomings. I had loving relationships and work that I cared about, but I couldn't feel content. Were my eyes sewn shut? How much longer could I pine for what was lost and could never be reclaimed, or, even worse, for some idealized perfect childhood that could never have been mine even if my parents had lived? I felt like the boy in Agee's novel *A Death in the Family:* "Everything was good and better than he could have hoped for, better than he ever deserved; only whatever it was and however good it was, it wasn't what you once had, and had lost, and could never have again. . . ." I tried to let go of what I had lost and be happy in what I had found.

I was cutting vegetables in the kitchen when Nick came in to ask how I was feeling. I'm well enough that I can act fine, I told him. "I don't care about how you act. I'm interested in how you feel." I'd never thought of my feelings as important to anyone who was depending on me. I'd been convinced that if I behaved right, didn't burden anybody, went about my duties and did what was expected, just like Mom, that was all the people I was close to wanted to see. I never anticipated that Nick's love for me would include my imperfections, painful feelings and all.

It was 1 A.M. and I was wide awake, as usual. I stared at Nick sleeping, then at Elizabeth, and it occurred to me that I was totally alone, that no one else could feel what I felt, that I could not be one with my mother, or allow her to live on inside me, that underneath the confusion about where I began and another person ended was a feeling of a terrible solitude I could not bear to face. My state of mind seemed so intolerable that my always-in-control-don't-want-to-impose-on-you manner broke down completely, and I called my friend Franny in the middle of the night. She talked to me for more than an hour, and came as close as anyone possibly could to letting me know that she could imagine what it was like to be inside my skin. I may indeed have been alone, but insofar as it was possible to reach across that gap and find comfort, I saw now that my adult life was as fortunate as my childhood was ill fated.

My episode of depression ended just as dramatically as it had begun. It was as if someone threw a switch. On February 26, 1980, I woke up to discover that my body and mind had returned. I had experienced firsthand what I already knew, that major depression is both a physical and a mental illness that bears no relationship to ordinary bad moods. It is severe but usually time-limited, with symptoms that run their course, and in most cases people eventually improve with or without treatment. The length of my depressive episode—eight months—was in the typical range. The more distance I gained from the episode, the more obvious it was to me that I had actually been physically ill.

I don't know why my depression stopped at this moment

any more than I know why it began at another. Was it the terror of separation reexperienced through my own daughter?
Was it because trying to get pregnant and have another child
frightened me so much? Could it be that a person can live in
the past just so long, and that someday the past catches up?
Was it punishment for having broken the promise I'd made to
myself long ago, never to reconnect to anyone again as
intensely as I had to my own mother, never to risk being
destroyed again by another loss? Or did it just happen to happen, a random chemical event?

What I know with great certainty is that the episode
changed my life permanently. It is probably the best and worst
thing that ever happened to me. The worst because I'm horrified that it is possible to suffer that much without being able
to gain the upper hand. To be that overwhelmed is weakness
in my view of the world, and I will never reclaim my sense of
perfect control. The best because I'm freer now. The pain of
all my losses came at me full force, and I did not die. My feelings have a new intensity, and I'm much less scared of them. I
know that my responses to real events can never be as frightening as my episode of depression.

I have read studies showing that maternal depression has a
negative impact on children. At first, this realization frightened me. What effect did my depression have on Elizabeth,
who was only twenty months old when my episode began? Yet
my relationship with Elizabeth became deeper and more honest when I accepted the terror and love that came with having a little girl of my own.

I've become a better psychiatrist as well. I now know the
terror of a psychiatric illness, and I have new respect for my
patients' fears of what lies below the surface of the stories they
tell me. I've learned how high the cost of discovery can be.

But most important, my adolescent anesthesia is gone. The wall I built around myself in my foster home, the wall that seemed so essential to my survival, has now fallen, and I accept being close to people again. I accept Nick's love, the love of a man who never deserted me during this terrible time, and my dreams that he'll leave me have ceased.

I never want to return to this place—the thought of it fills me with dread. Yet there's a part of it I also miss: the remarkable access to mysterious and powerful places that, no matter how I try, I cannot find again. But it is much better to be well. One such journey into the dark is enough.

I think about my own patients. I encounter colleagues who, like me, have also had depression and kept it secret. Almost no one has anything positive to say about major depression, and when an episode comes to an end, the patient is said to "return to baseline," the usual state of well-being. I cautiously asked a colleague who does research on depression: "Do you ever look at whether people return to a better place than baseline?" No, he answered, surprised by the question. Depression is not a growth experience but an illness, and only the vulnerable succumb. And yet for me, without this episode, I doubt I would ever have really confronted those feelings that stood in the way of my fully rejoining the world. The thought of it happening again is terrifying, and I am now convinced I will take any drug known to medical science if my depression recurs.

It has been shown that early loss in childhood increases the risk of depression. In fact, there is a powerful association between severe depression in adult women and the death of a mother in childhood. The association is stronger among poor girls than among the middle class, primarily because the poor are far less likely to receive adequate care following the mother's death. This in turn is associated with the likelihood of a negative self-image and poor adult life choices. Although neither my brother nor my sister has ever had it, maybe my own underlying vulnerability to major depression was unleashed by the events of my childhood. In any case, I am immensely grateful that the disease has so far never recurred.

Chapter 13

ANOTHER BEGINNING

(1983–1998)

A fter the episode of depression abated, my life returned to its normal routine, and I bid my therapist good-bye again, but a dull ache persisted, turning into acute torment every August on the anniversary of my mother's death, when the world seemed to fall apart again, at least the world as I understood it. And I wondered once more whether all my efforts had any purpose, what it meant that I was still here, and whom I might have harmed in my struggle for survival.

What happens when everything is fixed on the outside but still not right on the inside? The pain persists, despite obvious external indications of success, or maybe even because of them: it seems wrong to build a satisfying adult life on the foundation of all that suffering and death.

And then came the terrible paradox: if I couldn't permit myself to take pleasure in all that I had, then I needed to continue in a vain cycle in which I would strive for more, succeed, and then, still guilty, refuse to acknowledge that success. Destitute again, I would return once more to a painful state of feeling left out and envious. Yet I kept trying, kept believing that another achievement or another good deed would banish the terrible feelings I still had about myself. Professionally, I was engaged in nonstop activity, handling crises on the ward, seeing patients, teaching medical students and house staff, joining committees. Whatever anyone asked me to do, I did with enthusiasm. No additional task was too much, except when I was protecting my time with Elizabeth. When the workday ended, I would race home, excited to see her, obsessively attentive at every moment, trying to make up for the time I'd spent away from her. But neither my commitment to work nor my devotion to my daughter seemed enough to redeem me. I kept wondering whether a second child would make me feel whole, an internal debate tinged with despair.

I loved my time alone with Elizabeth, and I wanted to preserve it, protect our closeness. With two children, I might be overwhelmed, unsure how to divide myself between them. Suppose it's a boy and I act mean, the way Mom did with Henry. Would I be like the friend who once said to me, "I was a good mother to one child, but I'm doing terribly with two"? My connections to my own siblings still filled me with guilt. But didn't Elizabeth need a sibling? Wouldn't it be proof of my own inadequacy if I had only one? Isn't a second child insurance against the loss of the first? On the other hand, suppose

Nick died and I wound up all alone, just like Mom. Then wouldn't having one child be all that I could manage? Sometimes at night, tucking Elizabeth into bed, we would snuggle up close and I would silently wish that everything would remain the same, that she'd always be a little girl, unchanged by the passage of time. Yet I was enchanted by her developing skills, reassured by her increasing competence. If I loved one little child so much, why not have another? Round and round I went. Sometimes I was careless about birth control, thinking that if the child were an accident, maybe whatever went wrong would be excusable.

The accident never happened, and my obsession did not go away, so reluctantly I decided to seek a psychiatric consultation, to talk it through, maybe go for one or two sessions, and finally put the matter to rest. I wanted to see a woman, but who? This was the first time I was not a charity case, and what's more, I had inside information: this was a profession I was now a part of. But the freedom to choose only perplexed me, so I let my best friend Franny decide. She suggested one of her former supervisors, someone in our own department whom she admired but whom I hardly knew.

I was nervous when I called, on the one hand worried that this stranger would reject or frighten me, on the other convinced that she would have the instant solution to my problem. But she had no magic, good or bad, and it quickly became apparent that my obsession with having another child was just my latest version of self-torment, a reflection of my relentless dissatisfaction with myself, and a part of my fruitless search for an accomplishment that would "fix" me, that would undo the damage of my early losses and make me feel whole. It was beginning to dawn on me that either I would find an internal solution to my problem, or there would be no solution at all.

And so I wound up back in analysis. It was like an execution, I thought, contemplating the journey I was about to take through my inner life. My fear was intense.

My new analyst was Jewish and in her mid-fifties. She had a commanding presence, and she spoke English with an Austrian accent. I lay faceup on the couch in her small, sparely lit, soundproofed office. She listened silently, intently, out of sight behind me. All ordinary social discourse had become irrelevant. My mind wandered to the places in me where everything dangerous lurked: fear, pain, rage, lust, guilt, greed, untouched by the passage of time. Caution had kept me at a respectful distance from these places when I'd first set out on this path, but then, when my severe episode of depression made time stand still, I endured all my painful feelings at once, prayed that they would stop, waited while nature ran its course, and discovered that I could survive the confrontation after all. In the three years that followed, I had learned that there was no conscious way back to this terrifying place, and that the only territory I could explore lay outside, away from the volcanic center, where there were still footholds for safety. Now I was less afraid.

I set out on a journey amid the wreckage, searching for the words to describe a part of me, lost in time, the little girl who, using the evil magical powers that only children can fully believe they possess, committed the most odious crimes: destroyed my father and mother; betrayed my brother, usurping his role as the eldest child; stole my mother's baby Alexis and her boyfriend Sam; raised my sister badly; developed into a woman while my mother was deteriorating and becoming more like a man; failed to behave with my grandmother well enough so that she could cope with me; failed to want my aunts and uncles enough so that they would keep me; provoked my foster mother into a constant rage; and, worst of all, continued to live when I deserved to die.

My destructive powers were still with me—I was still a little girl who believed that something terrible would happen to anyone who got too close. I was poison. But in place of my younger sister depending on me, there was my daughter, and the possibilities seemed even more frightening. One small mistake and Elizabeth would die. I envisioned it a dozen times a day, my heart pounding. She gets a strep throat I fail to notice and it turns into rheumatic fever and her heart stops working. I feed her a piece of fruit and she chokes on it while I try in vain to revive her. I turn my head, she runs into the street, and a car runs over her. I'm picking her up from her piano lesson and she's kidnapped on the elevator on the way down from the teacher's apartment as I passively wait in the lobby. I had been involved in so much death that I sensed it lurking everywhere.

I'd made fatal mistakes, both long ago as a careless child and much later as a doctor. It is summer, a year after Mom died. Hot day, and the fire hydrants are turned on. We are spraying ourselves and the passing cars. I step down on the steaming pavement, and I don't see the little dog until he's right underfoot. He yelps in pain when I step on his front paw, and then runs into the street where he is hit by an oncoming car. He's terribly injured, probably dying, and the whole neighborhood gathers to sympathize with the owner and his crying, bleeding puppy. What happened? What scared him? No one saw, and I'm too chagrined and guilty to confess. An innocent puppy died because of my carelessness. I have never forgotten, and never forgiven myself.

232 CITY OF ONE

It is a quiet Sunday afternoon and I am the medical resident on call for the cancer ward. My new admission is a seventy-five-year-old woman, her small body wasted by disease, but her spirit diamond-hard. "I'm here to die," she announces. "I have pancreatic cancer, they gave me six months to live, and my time is up." Doctors are notorious for making pronouncements like this that never materialize, but this emaciated woman quite clearly has the look of death about her. "Do you have a family?" Oh, yeah, she's been married fifty years to a real bum, no kids. Since she's been sick, the old geezer's been driving her nuts with his demands. Well, now he can figure out for himself how to cook and clean, she announces triumphantly, because she's through with him. She's here to die alone; he's staying home.

I complete my evaluation, and since she asks for it, I order pain medication—two milligrams of Dilaudid intramuscularly, a standard dose of a typical narcotic. A few hours later, I find her in deep sleep. But then I notice the way she's breathing. It isn't the normal breathing of someone asleep. First a series of shallow breaths, then a sequence of increasingly deeper ones that slowly become shallower again, then no breaths at all, and the cycle starts again. I first learned about it in medical school, when a supervising resident told me to stay still and just watch. It is a pattern that has a name—Cheyne-Stokes respiration—and it is one of the heralds of death. I worry that the dose of narcotic I gave her was too much for her tiny, frail body, and now I stand at her bedside, contemplating my probable miscalculation. Even if I intervene now, she has at best a few days left. Is there anything to be gained by trying to extend her life for those few days, or should I honor her words and just let her be? I quietly walk away from her bedside, and by the next morning she has died. She is yet another patient on my conscience, one of many I have watched hovering in the ambiguous territory between life and death. Sometimes I act, sometimes I fail to, but neither action nor inaction seems right. I am not to be trusted.

Be forewarned, I told my new analyst: I nearly killed the last one. But she proceeded, unfazed and undeterred. Her Austrian descent became a theme in my dreams. In some, she was a casualty of the Holocaust who had lost her entire family. I wept for her. In others, she was a Nazi collaborator from whom I had to escape. Although I had no factual information whatever about this part of her life, these were the possibilities I'd invented for her: victim or victimizer.

Yet, as if there were no contradiction, my feelings for her were also warm and tender—she was like a mother, guarding the hearth, while I went out into the world secure in the knowledge of a safe haven when I returned. Her very existence felt like permission to try out the things I'd assiduously avoided. Mostly, she listened, and I made my own way.

I searched for the facts of my childhood only to discover that there were no facts to find, that I'd have to create my own coherent story. Did my father and grandfather adore me the way I adored them? Did my mother get any pleasure from her time with us, or was having children under such circumstances only a burden, and death a relief? Did our silence protect us, or did this inability to find words harm us further? What was my mother thinking when she sent Henry away? Did this abandonment serve as the model my aunts and uncles followed when they placed Alexis and me in foster care? And why couldn't my mother see the true character of her siblings? Did she really believe what she wrote to me about them in her deluded letter? I am unable to know what anyone else was thinking; I can shed no light on these mysteries.

Infrequently, summoning the courage to overcome my aversion, I would visit one or another of my aunts and uncles in my search for understanding. What was Mom expecting of you? Why did you send us away? I endured the discomfort of seeing them, but I learned nothing. Your mother was a very private person, they'd tell me. It was her dying wish that you and Alexis stay together. Erma and Jack had such a pretty place for you. We didn't have enough room, money, time, baby-sitters, space, furniture. We never did anything wrong. Why do you imply otherwise? Eventually, I gave up trying to figure out what really happened, and acknowledged that among the losses I must mourn are all the things I can never know and never understand.

I had adjusted to being left out, fatherless, even learned to make a virtue of it. At work, I was determined to defy those in authority. Confronted by powerful men, I was daring, challenging, filled with bravado. I spoke up, talked back, said whatever came to mind. What was there to lose that I hadn't lost already, and who needs a father anyway?

There were certain advantages to this. Freed from the necessity to please men, unfamiliar with the stereotypes dictating how mothers and fathers are supposed to behave, coming from a family in which the men had absented themselves for one reason or another, leaving the women to handle everything, I was unrestrained by the usual social conventions in these matters. I became one of the first women psychiatrists in my department to run an inpatient service, then an entire department with more than one hundred staff. I learned to do it all, to recruit staff, to negotiate a budget, to provide state-of-the-art treatment to hundreds of poor people who have severe mental illnesses.

But I'd also paid a price. I'd alienated the men who could potentially have helped me the most, shown them how difficult I could be, and that they had best keep their distance. I'd defended my service and its patients with great angry passion; I viewed every infringement on my mission as having life-and-death consequences; I was convinced—and I convinced those who worked most closely with me—that there was no way to compromise without abandoning the patients who were depending on us.

And there are real reasons to defend a program like mine. I complained to my analyst how little status the care of poor people has in a high-powered academic department of psychiatry, how I had to struggle to preserve the limited funds devoted to my service, surrounded by people preoccupied with other pursuits, barely aware of those who are today what I once was: left out, resourceless. One day, describing the vivid details of my latest battle with the departmental administration, she suggested that perhaps there was a way to accomplish my goals in a manner less injurious to me. At first I took her words as criticism, but I could also feel her genuine concern that I was harming myself, and I modified my approach. I gradually became more willing to negotiate calmly for what I needed, and less eager to be righteously offended.

As my passion for fighting with the men in power at work receded, I substituted my analyst as the target of my rage. Every negative expectation I'd ever had of those in authority, every disappointment I'd ever known, I now found in her behavior. She stood accused: for thinking badly of me, for wanting to harm me, for not listening, for lacking the compe-

tence to understand even when she did listen, for condoning
the behavior of everyone who ever hurt me, and then, worst
of all, for abandoning me every summer for a lengthy vacation, leaving me behind to suffer, indifferent to whether I
lived or died. She was never silent in the face of my attacks.
Remarkably, she empathized with the pain that motivated
them, and never retaliated or conceded that a crime had been
committed by either one of us. But she would need to prove
herself repeatedly before I finally came to believe she was really on my side. And I pressed on.

Freed from the feelings of daily outrage at work, I accepted
an invitation from my department chairman to give a talk at
a conference on schizophrenia, a disease I'd studied and treated for more than ten years. While I was aggressive and successful in fighting for my program, I'd shied away from any
public activity. Usually I was a member of the audience, but
now I was the speaker. I spent more than two hundred hours
preparing and writing my talk, then rehearsed it a dozen times.
I'd mastered my subject and memorized the speech, and I presented it before an audience of seven hundred professionals
and family members. It was lively, fluid, well organized; it
rolled off my tongue without a hitch. I finished. The audience
clapped. A fellow speaker asked how I had managed to present
all that information without even looking at my notes.
Parents approached me and told me the sad stories of their
grown sons and daughters with schizophrenia, their suffering,
their inability to make satisfying lives for themselves as a
result of their affliction with this incurable disease. I had no
answers for them.

Nick and Elizabeth came to pick me up. "How did it go?" I
explained the day's events, but in the back of my mind what I
was really thinking was, I want to die, I should just kill myself,

I don't deserve to be here, to be healthy, to be seen as a competent adult, to be applauded, to strive for success when I'm surrounded by so much misery.

Time passes. Things happen. Henry becomes a successful salesman, buys a pretty new condo, and moves his political opinions toward the right. He tries his best not to dwell on our unhappy past. Once in a while, we visit each other, searching for the commonalties that might define a sibling relationship severed so long ago. Alexis, after traveling widely, finally moves back to New York City. She makes and sells jewelry, and teaches English as a second language. We keep in touch, and while the painful feelings between us fade, it is difficult to rebuild the closeness we once had as small children. My foster siblings work, marry, and raise children. Erma takes in ever more stray cats and finds a job as an aide for disabled children. We show up for her holiday celebrations, the customary pandemonium. We each have our problems, but we "pass" in the adult world, indistinguishable from those who have never lived in foster care. I learn of Milton's death, which, despite my anger toward him, now seems only the sad ending to a story unresolved. Eventually, I lose track of my biological family completely. I am in my forties when Erma dies of cancer, and Jack survives only six months without her. Now our foster-family reunions are less frequent, although our feelings of affection remain.

In my own life I strive for continuity: same husband, daughter, friends, apartment, even the same dentist and dry cleaners and pizza place. At the hospital where I trained and have worked ever since, I have pieced together a splendid array of colleagues and mentors. I even have a permanent daytime spouse, my service's administrator. I've been with him almost as long as I've been with Nick, and since he's gay, our respective nighttime spouses are unthreatened and amused by our intimacy. It is as if after a childhood of uncertainty, I worked to put everything in place, constant and unchanging. But I could not control my analyst's comings and goings, and it astonished me that I found them so painful.

Every time she went on vacation, I felt like a helpless little girl again, convinced that my whole world was about to unravel. Despite all my attempts to be logical and rational and to remind myself that the past is past, every absence provoked another confrontation with my childhood. What if she disappears permanently just when I need her most, after she has accompanied me into the frightening territories of my own mind, places I would never be traversing without her? And why am I subjecting myself to a treatment that has the power to elicit such feelings repeatedly, a power no other real-life person or event seems to possess? I hate my dependence, I hate her leaving, I hate these repetitions, I hate watching myself spiral downward until everything starts to feel meaningless, as if her presence holds my life together and it will fall apart without her. I'm not good at this separation business.

"You're angry at me," she'd say simply, and she would wait. I had to keep rediscovering that it was true, that just below my despair lay helpless rage. If people I need could just come and go, then the only escape I had was to rid myself of needing them, to refuse to want what I could not control. But now that I had completed this internal rampage and momentarily allowed it to obliterate the importance of everything and everyone, the world seemed meaningless again, and present reality irrelevant. Just give me back what I lost, I'd tell my analyst. Be my real parent. You could if you wanted to. Now I was digging myself in, childlike, insisting that she had the magic to undo the past that I felt unable to concede could not be undone. Finally, when I understood how painful this way of protecting myself was, and how angry her desertion made me feel, I saw I was nevertheless still connected, that my terrible feelings had not destroyed our bond.

"But I don't want to be connected," I told her, recalling my recurrent childhood nightmare of being glued to the floor of the bus, trapped, no escape. "You'll come and go no matter what I do or say, and when you leave you'll take everything that's good between us with you."

"Once I'm gone," she responded, "you'll find that your good feelings about us are still within you." Could I really find what I need inside me? She acted as though I had the resources to heal myself, refusing to accept what to me seemed the obvious truth: that my losses had catastrophically harmed me. She rejected my insistence that I was unimportant, and in the face of my tirades about meaninglessness, she confronted me with the enduring commitments I had to my work, family, and friends. I'd spent a long time detailing my flaws and failures, and she had listened carefully. And then one day she shocked me by presenting an uncharacteristically long narrative citing every piece of evidence to the contrary, every detail of my personal and professional accomplishments that I had refused to acknowledge. She knew me so well that it was impossible to dispute her account. She helped me see how my sense of failure protected me from confronting my guilt over what I had, my fear of losing it, the irony of finding success as painful as it was pleasurable. How was I to live with the facts: that my mother was poor and ill and widowed, and that I was well off and healthy and loved? Didn't I have to atone for the crimes I had committed, and relinquish what I didn't deserve to have? She challenged my insistence on my destructive powers, my refusal to acknowledge my childhood helplessness, my belief that there was just so much good fortune to go around in the world, and that what I had must have been unfairly taken from others. And she returned after every separation unharmed and unchanged. Encouraged by her perspective, I continued on, and the feelings of despair and self-loathing that followed each success gradually diminished.

I gave more talks, published professional papers, and obtained grants to do my own teaching and research. And I had a hidden advantage. Nick had moved away from teaching to his true vocation as a writer and editor, and every paper I wrote and every talk I gave we worked on together. It was like a childhood dream come true, a replacement for the father I had lost who would have helped me succeed in the world. With total support and no signs of competition, Nick showed me how to use half as many words to convey twice as much meaning, spending hours helping me say what I wanted to say to the world.

One day, preparing a talk on delivering mental health care to indigent patients, I decided I would include among my slides a few images from my own past. I packed my camera and climbed into the hospital van to drive with Wally to the South Bronx. It was the weekend of the L.A. riots in 1992, when the word was that for white people in big cities, the best place to be was at home. Even Wally wondered if it was a good idea, but we had arranged this outing weeks ago and I didn't know when I'd have another chance. Besides, I said to Wally, who's going to bother me, walking around with a 260-pound black guy? It had been fifteen years since I was last in the

South Bronx, and little of what I knew was left. The abandoned buildings I found on my last visit were now mostly torn down, replaced by vacant lots or two-story industrial structures. My once bustling neighborhood was a ghost town. Ruby's fruit stand was now some sort of warehouse. My first apartment building was a patch of concrete under the Cross Bronx Expressway, my second a grassy plot of land with a few abandoned cars rusting nearby. Not much to photograph, but I pointed the camera and snapped anyway. Then finally I saw something familiar: the little tombstone store on Washington Avenue and 176th Street, just as it was when I was a child and wondered who might be buried there. Everything else from my old neighborhood may have disappeared, but death, apparently, survived. "Look, Wally! That place is exactly the same as when I was a kid." Wally looked at me, bemused. We climbed into the van.

During the ride back, we discussed one of our usual topics: Wally's love life. "I'm not good at love," he said, referring to his passionate but rocky domestic life with a woman he adored but did not trust. When you grow up like we did, I remind him, it's hard to be good at love.

Wally likes to call me his psychiatrist, though he rarely follows any of my advice. Still, I discover I'm drawn to mulling over the strategies couples use to solve their conflicts, and I decide to start to treat them in my practice. Working with couples reminds me of my efforts to mediate between Mom and Henry, and I find myself equally sympathetic to both sides of the story, unperturbed by the contradictions in the separate realities presented to me, trying only to clarify one party's version to the other and help them discover a less painful truth. I know what it is like to fight instead of facing internal despair, and what it means to firmly and falsely believe that someone else holds the secret to the resolution of one's pain.

For me, professional success meant competition with men, but my relationships with women were another matter entirely. Here I refused to acknowledge anger or conflict. I denied that I competed with other women for anything—for a man, for power, for success. I had irreparably harmed my mother, and it was just too dangerous.

But Elizabeth finds it easier to face difficult feelings, and my relationship with her is a source of wonder. We have the empathy I felt with my mother, but we also have words, and the words allow us to be both close and separate in ways I never knew with Mom. When Elizabeth was eight, she phoned home from a Halloween sleep-over. I didn't tell her that her pet turtle had just died because I didn't want to spoil her fun. "Never do that again! You have to tell me! As soon as it happens!" The following year, she stumbled on evidence of my previous marriage and was shocked and hurt that I'd kept this from her. I remained unsure about what was sensible to share with a child, but I did nothing to censor Elizabeth's running commentary about my parenting skills. I listened, accepting the perceptive critique, astounded by the oscillations in her feelings about me—admiration and devotion at one moment, disappointment and detestation the next. I was forced to admit that my own feelings were not so simple either. And I was stunned by her willingness to acknowledge our rivalry.

My competition with Elizabeth emerged as worry and panic. "Elizabeth got a 68 on a math test!" I told my analyst, as if my daughter had just been diagnosed with a terminal illness. I was great at math as a kid, and I feared that any contest I won against Elizabeth was proof that one day I would harm her, fatally, just like Mom.

"What's so tragic about getting a 68 on a math test?" my analyst asked. I was shocked by her question. Wasn't it obvious? But I guess it wasn't so obvious after all. Why focus on what's wrong when so much is right, when Elizabeth is warm and beautiful and gifted with talents I never had?

Competition with my daughter proved too frightening, so I competed with my analyst instead. She was safer. Who's smarter or richer or slimmer or prettier or more successful or better dressed or has a better man? And yes, I learned to admit that I did compete with women, even if I still carried around my irrational fear that such competition was deadly, as it was when I was growing in strength while Mom was losing everything: her breast, her boyfriend Sam, my baby sister Alexis. I was the victor, left with the spoils.

Months passed, then years, and all my carrying on not only left my analyst and me uninjured but created a powerful bond between us. I'd never before had such an indestructible caretaker, someone as relentless in her belief in our constructive power as I was in our power to destroy, someone who firmly held that we would both survive while I was convinced that we were doomed.

Gradually I developed an inner structure that did not fall apart in times of stress or separation, one that reminded me of the buildings my brother and I used to make with his Erector set, lining up the strips of metal until a sturdy structure was in place that couldn't be knocked over. Slowly I came to see that we were safe. Reluctantly, I gave up my belief in my powers and admitted that my crimes were the fantasies of a child who found the alternatives even worse; that all my rage was impotent; that I watched my mother gradually deteriorate even though she was all I had to depend on; that I only thought I could stop her from dying because I couldn't possibly cope with such a frightening reality; that nevertheless she was going to die and there was nothing I could do about it. And that my aunts and uncles were adults, who would make their own decisions for their own reasons, and that I had no power over them either. But I also learned that I was no longer that small helpless child. Eventually, and to my great surprise, my feelings of anger and disappointment diminished and my sense of meaninglessness faded away, disappeared altogether.

"But I hate ordinary reality," I protested. "I prefer my childhood magic." I know from my own psychiatric training that the belief that one is in command, a so-called internal locus of control, is one of the few personal traits that consistently correlates with increased resilience, an ability to bounce back from adversity and continue on. This is reassuring, because God knows I possess this trait in abundance. But as I let it register that the emergency was over, I now found relief in acknowledging what was really possible. I admit that I cannot be one with another person, cannot "fix" what someone else feels. At best, it may be possible to help people fix themselves. So I learn how to feel for my patients without trying to join them. I accept that we are each in some sense alone. I understand how to get past the guilt that another's suffering is not my own—that I am not my mother. And when Elizabeth turned eleven, the age at which I was orphaned, I was surprised to discover that instead of feeling lost with no model for a parent-child relationship, I felt liberated, free to make my own choices about how to be a good mother, free to move on from my own painful childhood. I'd invent it from here on, and the thought contained the hope for something better.

My memories of my mother were constant, vivid, but I remembered so little about my father that I felt only the indirect effects of his loss—my mother's struggle to manage without him, my belief that any man who loved me would desert me, my dismissive attitude toward powerful men, expressed for years in my anger and bravado, my fantasies of preserving Dad within me by being manly. I was unable to reconcile any of this with my husband's trustworthiness and consistency.

"How do you explain Nick?" my analyst asked. I don't explain him, I responded. That relationship is a fluke, an accident, dumb luck. But gradually I became willing to consider how I had patched the pieces together to make it happen—my fragmented memories of the love between Dad and me, my adoration of Grandpa and Sam, the long list of male doctors and teachers I admired, the confidence I gained from the male therapist who treated me, my painful struggle to permit a man to take a central place in my life, a role I had long reserved for my dying mother. Whatever the explanation, I grew convinced of my more tender feelings for men, and with that, of the diamond-hard permanence of my relationship with Nick.

I now began to feel less dismissive of my father, and more interested in his history. I took a trip to Wayne State University in Detroit, where the Walter P. Reuther Library of Labor and Urban Affairs holds the transcript of the 1918 Industrial Workers of the World sedition trial. For two days, from the time the library opened in the morning until it closed at night, I skimmed the entire transcript of my father's trial—thousands of pages of material, the complete testimony of more than a hundred defendants, discussing the hardships of miners, migrant farmers, and construction workers in the early twentieth century, and the techniques the IWW had used to organize them.

After hours of reading, I finally reached the page where my father took the stand. "Do you have anything to say?" the judge asked him. "No," he responded, and the judge dismissed

him. That's it? I've come a thousand miles seventy years later
and spent two days reading through this turgid transcript, and
that's all you have to say? I'm muttering, aloud, irrationally
irritated, as if Dad should have anticipated this moment. But
whatever disappointment I felt in his terseness, I was proud
that I had a father who was willing to sacrifice for principle,
and I felt more willing to credit his importance to me.

It was 1991, eleven years since my episode of depression
ended, and eight since my analysis began. Often I had a sense
of inner peace, a feeling which astounded me. Yet there were
still two events that I still could not tolerate: the return of
summer, and traveling to an unfamiliar place. The onset of
warm weather transported me to the season in which both my
parents died, and my analyst's vacations plus the routine sum-
mertime comings and goings of colleagues and friends intensi-
fied the dread. Even more remarkable was that after months of
feeling well, all it took was an airplane flight to an unfamiliar
city to leave me uprooted, dislocated, a lost child. I was transformed into a helpless thirteen-year-old on that stomach-
churning journey to my foster home. I began to feel physically ill, nauseated, dizzy, and exhausted. A fog separated me
from the world, and I didn't want to be in a new place. On
vacations, I hid my feelings so I wouldn't ruin anyone else's
good time. On business trips, I struggled to meet my obliga-
tions. When I could, I forestalled the problem by avoiding
travel altogether. My list of excuses was endless.

But there was no avoiding summer. As my state of mind
improved, my tolerance for the periods of suffering decreased.
So now I thought about antidepressants. There was a new
one—Prozac—that was much easier to tolerate than the ones
I'd learned to prescribe during my training. I'd seen some of
my own patients improve dramatically on it, and yet I was still

wary about taking it myself. Why give in now when I've held out this long, when I was already so much better? "I could replace you this summer with a pill," I jauntily told my analyst, trusting that she'd assure me that it was a terrible idea.

"Why not take medication if you'll suffer less?" she said. Astonishing. I thought of my suffering as a necessary part of staying attached, an essential form of remembering, but she thought our relationship could go on without it. Moreover, I'd moved closer to her view that I was not so damaged after all, and it seemed possible that taking medicine would not constitute proof that I was defective. I went to a psychopharmacologist for a consultation, and we agreed to proceed. One hot July day, I emptied the contents of a Prozac capsule into a glass of orange juice, carefully preparing my witch's brew. Then I measured out a small amount of the juice into another glass, so that the drink now contained only a fraction of the medicine in the original capsule. Then I stared at the glass, fearful that this was either an admission of defeat or, worse, the beginning of an irreversible transformation. But I was tired of suffering, and I swallowed it.

Even the tiny dose I had taken was barely tolerable—I lost my appetite and couldn't sleep. It would be a long time before I reached an optimal dosage, but from the outset I noticed something dramatic. There now seemed to be a net beneath me, proof against a disastrous fall. Summer came and produced only a mild change in my sense of well-being. I could enjoy traveling. My horizons expanded. I gave professional talks in unfamiliar places and looked for opportunities to travel for pleasure. This felt so alien that I might even have concluded that it was not really me, but instead I decided that it was me in an improved version. Far from replacing my analyst or dampening my emotional responses, the medicine allowed me to feel freer to explore both my inner life and the outer world. It provided another assurance that the depression would not return. When mild symptoms now come and go, I think of them as the small scars marking the place that was once a festering wound.

The medicine had another effect I did not predict. My anticipation of disaster greatly diminished. Is Nick late tonight because he has been shot dead by a mugger and is lying in a pool of blood on a deserted street? Has Elizabeth failed to call by ten o'clock because she was hit by a car and now lies comatose in a hospital bed, with no papers to identify her? My ability to generate thoughts like this and then feel panicked by them had remained intact through all my years of analysis. Now the thoughts still crossed my mind, but much less often, and when they did, it was easier to dismiss them as unlikely or unrealistic.

Still I had to contend with August 29. The anniversary of my mother's death remained the most terrible day of the year, dread in the anticipation, cold fear in the experience. I had to be absolutely wide awake on this day to life's routine dangers—driving a car, crossing the street, choosing an airplane flight—lest I die or cause the death of someone I loved. In this day's solemnity, all routine pleasure had to be forsworn. If I dared to relax, I invited fate to take its revenge on a little girl who was busy playing while her mother lay dying.

But on this August 29, I woke up and was surprised that I felt well. After years of conscious effort, although from some deeply unconscious place, it occurred to me that this would be a good day to celebrate my mother's life, rather than mourn her death. I was grateful for our years together, for the importance of each day, for the skills she taught me, for all the other women who had mothered me, for the analyst-mother who had helped me reconstruct my inner world. And when I reached the age my mother was when she died, instead of guilt I felt freedom and gratitude. These are extra years now, a gift of life beyond what I ever expected, and I am thankful to have them.

I do not miss my fantasies of catastrophe. A chance for ordinary adult happiness is enough for me now. I once imagined that the ordinary would be boring, or at least a kind of defeat, a failure to reclaim the most desirable but now lost original, a second-best alternative accepted only because it is realistic and possible. But the ordinary turns out to be wonderful, even magical. It is the pleasure of daily life with a man who has shown me how reliable someone I love can really be. It is having a daughter who has grown into a delightful and competent adult, proving that mother and child can survive and prosper. It is letting go of the impossible only to find that the possible is nevertheless of great value, that my patients and projects at work provide me with unending satisfaction. It is integrating the past, the pain and losses of childhood, with a present marked by the successes of adult life. It is living in a world that is solid, and not about to fall apart. It is a feeling of repair and inner peace, the end of a tortuous route from the comfort of my first home as a small child, through the years of unraveling and destruction, to the creation of a second secure base, established after great effort and with considerable help from others. Although it once seemed unlikely, it has happened. I have found my way home.

EPILOGUE

(1998)

On May 2, 1997, I am driving home. The news is on the radio. "A forty-eight-year-old New Jersey man was killed today while driving his son home from a baseball game when a tree struck his car during a thunderstorm. His six-year-old son was uninjured." Uninjured! I begin to imagine the thoughts of this uninjured six-year-old: If only we'd taken another road . . . If only we had left earlier . . . If only I hadn't played baseball today . . . Why Dad and not me? And then I think of the tenacious resistance against acknowledging the irreversibility of the loss, the haunting ways in which the event will replay itself throughout his life. I imagine him twenty-five years from now, driving his own son home from a baseball game, caught in a thunderstorm, reminded of the horror of seeing his father crushed under a tree. He is just starting out, this uninjured six-year-old, and he has no idea yet what the world holds in store for him.

Most adults find a child's grief so painful to contemplate and difficult to confront that they prefer to believe it doesn't exist, that the child simply doesn't understand. Yet while children do not articulate their needs in the ways adults do, they are far from oblivious. They watch, worry, observe the behavior of the adults around them, perceive that they are being left out or underestimated, contain the feelings they judge too dangerous to express. They pass judgment, censor their speech, feel powerless and powerful at once. They take responsibility for, and feel guilty about, developments in their lives that are in fact largely out of their control. They invent theories to explain what is happening to them, and believe that whatever happened before, however unlikely it may have been, is bound to happen again. All this I know from my own experience.

It is not easy to understand the complex amalgam of strengths and weaknesses of children who have experienced multiple losses in childhood. Independence and precociousness, developed out of necessity, can disguise a multitude of deprivations, weaknesses, and profound needs, even in the small number of children who seem to have found adequate substitute parents. It takes much time, effort, and money to repair what has gone wrong.

Ignoring children's perceptions and overlooking the complexity and sophistication of their thoughts is one danger. Another is to assume that because they have reached the age of emancipation, they have developed the skills that will ensure adult success or happiness. It is unrealistic to believe that children who have had no solid grounding in the first place can suddenly become capable adults simply because they have reached the legal age of eighteen.

Time alone does not, alas, heal all wounds. In fact, it can be extremely difficult to rebuild a sense of trust in the future after a childhood marked by separation and loss. In many ways, I grew up in a fortunate time and place. Various kinds of public assistance—low-cost housing, low-cost health care, free education through college—allowed me to keep going. A significant amount of public money was invested in me, and I hope that in some way the dividends have been paid, the bond redeemed. In America today, where one in five children lives below the government-defined poverty line, and where the AIDS epidemic has radically increased the number of orphans, there is good reason to wonder whether today's parentless children will be given the same chance to survive and prosper that I was given. In fact, there is considerable doubt as to whether these children in need can find, anywhere, the kind of help that was essential to my recovery.

When a parent dies, what remains is an internal relationship with the absent mother or father, a relationship that seems all the more important to preserve and carry forward when there are no suitable substitutes. Part of that relationship involves creating a coherent story, clarifying the medical facts and psychological experiences. This narrative can be a tool, a key to mastery. But each person's story is different, and it is easy to draw the wrong conclusions from any single account. My central purpose is not to inspire with a story of triumph over tragedy, however flattered or pleased I will be if anyone has found that here, but to provide useful information based on both scientific knowledge and my own experience which can help those personally and professionally concerned to understand the difficult and dangerous journey that lies ahead of a child whose parents have died.